Animal Theory

Animal Theory

A Critical Introduction

Derek Ryan

EDINBURGH
University Press

Edinburgh University Press Ltd
The Tun – Holyrood Road
12(2f) Jackson's Entry
Edinburgh EH8 8PJ

www.euppublishing.com

Typeset in 11/13 Ehrhardt by
Servis Filmsetting Ltd, Stockport, Cheshire,
and printed and bound in Great Britain by
CPI Group (UK) Ltd, Croydon CR0 4YY

A CIP record for this book is available from the British Library

ISBN 978 0 7486 8219 5 (hardback)
ISBN 978 0 7486 8221 8 (webready PDF)
ISBN 978 0 7486 8220 1 (paperback)
ISBN 978 0 7486 8222 5 (epub)

Contents

Acknowledgements

First and foremost I would like to thank Jackie Jones at Edinburgh University Press for initially suggesting the idea of a critical introduction to animal theory. I am extremely grateful to her for placing confidence in me, and for her encouragement as the project began to take shape. My thanks also to Jackie's colleagues at EUP and to my two anonymous reviewers.

This book has been enriched by conversations with a number of friends, colleagues and animal studies scholars over the past few years. I am especially thankful to Ariane Mildenberg, John Miller, Kaori Nagai, Jane Spencer, Vicki Tromanhauser and Sarah Wood for generously giving time to read and comment on chapters or sections of my typescript as it was nearing completion. For sharing insights, I would also like to thank Judith Allen, Claire Davison, Jeanne Dubino, Jane Goldman, Matt Hayler, Donna Landry, Michael Lawrence, Laci Mattison, Laura McMahon, Caroline Pollentier, Maria Ridda, Kath Swarbrick, Lynn Turner and Ben Worthy. I am grateful to the organisers and delegates of various energising and fascinating animal studies conferences and events I have attended in recent years, in particular 'Queer/Animal' (King's College London, 2012), 'Cosmopolitan Animals' (University of Kent, 2012) and 'Reading Animals' (University of Sheffield, 2014). And many thanks to those who attended the University of Kent's Student Forum on 'Eating Animals', as well as to the students who attended my 'Revolutionary Animals' Summer School session at Kent's Paris campus, which partly inspired the opening to this book.

Finally, a very special thank you to my family for their continued love, support and interest in my work.

Για την Στέλλα

Introduction

Nénette, Théodora, Tamü and Joey are Borneo orang-utans. They weigh approximately 100 kg and measure 1.4 m in height. Their 'home' is the rainforest. They are 'people of the forest'.

Each year half a million visitors stand in front of a sign detailing four primates housed in the centre of Paris. A relatively small zoo, it nonetheless offers the opportunity to see 1,800 animals of almost 200 species, from invertebrates to amphibians, birds to reptiles, fish to mammals. For most people the zoo presents an opportunity to encounter an array of exotic animals from around the world that they would otherwise likely never see in the flesh. In contrast to looking at animals on a television, on a computer screen, or in the pages of a book, the only thing between the animal inside the enclosure and the human standing outside is glass or bars and a sign that provides information about length and weight, habitat and height: the blue poison dart frogs are 5 cm long and their home is the tropical forests of northern Brazil; the Arabian camels weigh 650 kg and their home is the desert in northern Africa and southeastern Asia; the snow leopard weighs 55 kg and measures 1.30 m long and its home is the mountain ranges of central and southern Asia; the axolotl, 30 cm and 110 g, finds its home in Mexico's Lake Xochimilco. Yet encounters between humans and animals in zoos – regardless of the information provided and the closeness in proximity – are often marked by a sense of distance and distraction. Inside the enclosures the parrots perch too perfectly still; the foxes gather in the far corner; the small tortoises scratch at the glass. Outside, we glance and point and shuffle, moving promptly from one enclosure to the next. The orang-utans turn their backs on us and we turn our backs on them.

Founded in 1793, the Ménagerie du Jardin des Plantes is the world's oldest civil zoo. In the midst of the French Revolution, opposition grew towards the

private menageries of exotic animals that had been reserved for the aristoc-
racy. The display of animals as part of various private collections, travelling
shows or circuses could no longer be justified (although to this day many do,
of course, remain); in their place, the vision was for a new public zoological
garden that would be open to all and free to access. For the writer and botanist
Jacques-Henri Bernardin de Saint-Pierre it was an opportunity for scientists
to learn about animals by observing their behaviour live; for others it was a
chance to domesticate exotic creatures, to educate the general public or to
bring economic prosperity (Baratay and Hardouin-Fugier 2003: 75). The
captivation of exotic animals would no longer benefit the status of elite individuals, but instead cities and nations seeking to display their colonial might
(Ritvo 1987: 232; Berger 2009: 31). Influenced by the success in Paris, zoological gardens emerged in major cities throughout the nineteenth century, from
London to Dublin, Amsterdam to Copenhagen, Berlin to Brussels. Admission
rates soared. In the twentieth century the number of large zoos in Europe grew
from fifty at the beginning to over 300 at the end of the century (the many
more small zoos would vastly increase these figures), with an estimated 150
million visitors each year (Baratay and Hardouin-Fugier 2003: 230; 203). With
this growth in zoos, large and small, replicated across other continents, there
are now in excess of 10,000 worldwide, with an estimated 700 million visitors
each year. As this shift has developed from private menageries to public zoos,
the purpose and scope of these spaces has also changed. Gradually the scientific ambitions of the zoos have been undermined by the limited life expec-
tancy of captivated animals, high mortality rates, the belief that the conditions
distort the behaviour of animals and the sense that studying individual animals
can't be accurately representative of entire species. The idea that zoos can help
preserve species under threat of extinction and return them to the wild has
also been of more limited success than is commonly believed (Jamieson 2006:
139–40). The disappointment in such scientific goals has led to zoos instead
turning their focus to education and entertainment of the public (Baratay and
Hardouin-Fugier 2003: 123; 131; 146).

   And yet, there is a sense that zoos are disappointing to those seeking to be
educated and entertained, too. What do we learn about animals through the
facts and figures on display outside their cages? On average visitors to zoos only
remain in front of each enclosure for between thirty seconds to two minutes
(Mullan and Marvin 1999: 133; DeMello 2012: 111), the signs and labels next
to these enclosures are not widely read (DeMello 2012: 109–10), and zoo-goers
frequently display similar prejudices about animals to those who never visit
(Jamieson 2006: 135). How much do we really enjoy visits to the zoo? The
Guardian recently reported that London Zoo was under investigation after
'revelations of alcohol-fuelled incidents' during special 'Zoo Lates' sessions
that run on Friday nights from 6–10 pm in the summer and are described on

the website as 'London's Wildest Night Out!' The incidents – which included 'a beer being thrown over a tiger, a drunken woman reportedly trying to enter a lion enclosure and a man stripping off and attempting to enter the penguin pool' (Vaughan 2014) – may not be the norm when it comes to the behaviour of zoo visitors, but the story does offer a particularly troubling example of how far the drive to entertain can become removed from the lives and interests of the animals. More sober daily visits to zoos are often met with a quieter sense of disappointment, a phenomenon described by John Berger in his groundbreaking essay 'Why Look at Animals?':

> The animals seldom live up to the adults' memories, whilst to the children they appear, for the most part, unexpectedly lethargic and dull. (As frequent as the calls of animals in a zoo are the cries of children demanding: Where is he? Why doesn't he move? Is he dead?) And so one might summarize the felt, but not necessarily expressed, question of most visitors as: Why are these animals less than I believed? . . . Visitors visit the zoo to look at animals. They proceed from cage to cage, not unlike visitors in an art gallery who stop in front of one painting, and then move on to the next or the one after next. Yet in the zoo the view is always wrong. Like an image out of focus. One is so accustomed to this that one scarcely notices it any more. (2009: 33)

Berger raises an important question about not only the kinds of encounters we have with animals but also what kinds of animals we really encounter in zoos. For 'however you look at these animals, even if the animal is up against the bars, less than a foot from you, looking outwards in the public direction, *you are looking at something that has been rendered absolutely marginal*; and all the concentration you can muster will never be enough to centralize it' (34). Not only are the scientific merits of zoos overstated, but the benefits of containing animals for education and entertainment are also exaggerated.

A paradox emerges whereby the development of public zoos characterises both the human interest in, and exploitation of, animals. Jacques Derrida provides one explanation for this in *The Beast and the Sovereign*, when he reflects on how he remains 'enamoured of the Jardin des Plantes' (2009: 275) while at the same time pointing to how such zoos continue to be based on problematic power structures:

> one moves from luxury and useless expense, one transitions from sumptuary beasts to useful beasts, to a viable and profitable menagerie: profitable to knowledge but also profitable . . . to economy . . . in this reform of the zoo, the zoological garden, and the zoological in general, not to speak . . . of circuses and private houses . . . [we see] taming,

training, stock raising, so many modalities of master and sovereign power . . . possession, appropriation, and the property of beasts (through capture, hunting, raising, commerce, enclosure). (283)

The transfer to public zoo from private menagerie failed to address the exploitation of animals because the latter's 'reality' was 'destroyed' without 'deconstructing the model'. Derrida calls this model 'autopsic' in that it neutralises and objectifies nonhuman life, 'de-vitalises' animals, and 'consists in enclosing, depriving of freedom of movement and, hence, of freedom itself, hence of power, of power to see, to know, to have beyond certain limits, and hence of sovereignty' (296; 300). Derrida's long-standing concern with animality, and especially his later work such as *The Animal That Therefore I Am* and both volumes of *The Beast and the Sovereign*, abundantly demonstrates that deconstructing these power relations is a task that requires a fundamental shift in our theoretical models. The 'revolutionary' shift from private to public collections of animals has not really changed the treatment of animals for the better, or challenged the perceived divide between human and animal, because it has not been met with a sufficient revolution *in thought*.

Animal Theory is not strictly speaking a book about zoos, but it is a book about encountering many animals in thought. Visiting zoos opens up the question of how we come to meet animals in the modern world and, crucially, what we do and don't think about during such encounters. For between humans and animals – whether those in zoos, the pets we share everyday experiences with, or the meat that ends up on our tables – there is a long history of thinking about animals as lacking in the kind of capacities or value that humans are judged to have. Many people leave the zoo without their assumptions about the divide between humans and animals having been seriously challenged, yet what really creates the species barrier is not simply some unbridgeable difference between (our) humanity and (their) animality but rather the nature of the encounter itself. In zoos, what is between these nonhuman animals and human visitors – the facts and figures, glass and bars – symbolically and materially marks the asymmetry of such inter-species meetings which depend on nonhuman animals that have been captured, categorised and caged by humans. By turning to attempts to theorise animals and animality, this book explores what is between this apparent divide. It seeks to better understand the asymmetrical way we have encountered animals in thought so as to better understand how we encounter animals in life.

A HISTORY OF ANTHROPOCENTRISM? ANTIQUITY AND ENLIGHTENMENT

The history of western philosophy presents many examples of animals caged in anthropocentric – that is, human-centred – modes of thought that have had a dominant influence on thinking about the capacities of animals, how they should be treated, and how they are commonly judged to be lower in status than humans (or, to be more precise, 'man'). In order to understand the philosophical inheritance passed on to the various thinkers this book engages with, it is important to look back to two hugely significant periods of development in theorising animals and animality: Ancient Greece, where classical philosophers first began systematically to consider animal life; and seventeenth-century Europe, when a line of philosophers influenced the Enlightenment by turning away from tradition and faith, and towards science and reason, in their efforts to understand the human's place in nature. These two periods in philosophy are crucial not only because they reveal the anthropocentric assumptions that would become widely influential in shaping the way nonhuman life would be conceptualised and treated, but also because in them we find the often marginalised voices that open up the possibility of a thinking which is not centred on humanity. Contained within the history of anthropocentric thought is the beginnings of an alternative history of less- or even *non*-anthropocentric approaches to animals and animality.

Minds and Machines

In his *Politics*, Aristotle (384–322 BCE) presents the much-cited statement that 'man' is separated from other animals because he 'is by nature a political animal' (1995: 10). What Aristotle means by this is that man finds his natural flourishing in the *polis* or 'city-state' where his capacity for language, reason and ethical judgement sets him apart from nonhuman life. To be sure, some animals may form their own kind of common societies, but man is

> in a higher degree than bees or other gregarious animals . . . man alone
> of the animals is furnished with the faculty of language. The mere
> making of sounds serves to indicate pleasure and pain, and is thus a
> faculty that belongs to animals in general: their nature enables them to
> attain the point at which they have perceptions of pleasure and pain,
> and can signify those perceptions to one another. But language serves
> to declare what is advantageous and what is the reverse, and it is the
> peculiarity of man, in comparison with other animals, that he alone
> possesses a perception of good and evil, of the just and the unjust, and

other similar qualities; and it is association in these things which makes a family and a city. (11)

Language, reason and ethical judgement serve to elevate man above the experience of pleasure and pain. Aristotle therefore sees a natural hierarchical relation between man and animal where intelligence is more important than bodily capacities: 'there must necessarily be a union of the naturally ruling element with the element which is naturally ruled, for the preservation of both. The element which is able, by virtue of its bodily power, to do the physical work, is a ruled element, which is naturally in a state of slavery' (8). With direct reference to animals he adds that this same natural principle holds true, where 'tame animals have a better nature than wild, and it is better for all such animals that they should be ruled by man because they then get the benefit of preservation'. Aristotle's repeated use of 'man' is telling, since within and between animal kinds he views 'the relation of male to female' to be 'naturally that of the superior to the inferior, of the ruling to the ruled' (16). His view of animals is that they, like women, live to serve man: 'Plants exist for the benefit of animals, and some animals exist for the benefit of others' (23). In antiquity it seems that you must either be a man or exist for the benefit of one.

In modern Europe, by far the most influential statement about animals is attributed to René Descartes' *Discourse on Method*, first published in 1637, which divides thinking humans from automated animals. '*I think, therefore I am*' is 'the first principle' of Cartesian philosophy, and the only beings with access to this 'I', which is the mind 'entirely distinct from body', are human (1968: 53–4). In a notorious passage which captures the view of a split between mind and body, human and animal, Descartes writes:

if there were such machines which had the organs and appearance of a monkey or of some other irrational animal, we would have no means of recognizing that they were not of exactly the same nature as these animals: instead of which, if there were machines which had a likeness to our bodies and imitated our actions, inasmuch as this were morally possible, we would still have two very certain means of recognizing that they were not, for all that, real men. Of these the first is, that they could never use words or other signs, composing them as we do to declare our thoughts to others . . . And second is that, although they might do many things as well as, or perhaps better than, any of us, they would fail, without doubt, in others, whereby one would discover that they did not act through knowledge, but simply through the disposition of their organs: for, whereas reason is a universal instrument which can serve on any kind of occasion, these organs need a particular disposition for each particular action; whence it is that it is morally impossible to have enough different organs in a machine to make it act in all the occurrences of life in the same way as our reason makes us act. (73–4)

As with Aristotle, we see the emphasis here on rational 'men' who have access to language and knowledge set against the 'irrational animal'. For Descartes, all animals are considered lesser than even 'the most unintelligent men' (74). Echoing the view of man as a political animal who flourishes through his wide-ranging role in society, the Cartesian man is intelligent enough to communicate and learn multiple things. Entirely overlooking any possibility that the utterances of 'magpies and parrots' can be an example of signs that express *meaning*, or a kind of thought, and overlooking those humans who for whatever reason cannot speak, Descartes concludes that 'there are no men so dull-witted and stupid, not even imbeciles, who are incapable of arranging together different words, and of composing discourse by which to make their thoughts understood' and that 'there is no other animal, however perfect and whatever excellent disposition it has at birth, which can do the same'. The lines drawn by Descartes are firm and clear; it is 'not only that animals have less reason than men, but that they have none at all', 'they do not have a mind' (74–6). Caught up in this split between the immortal soul of man and the automated functions of the body, the animal is trapped in a definition of all that the human is not.

Anthropocentrism (and androcentrism, given that 'men' so often stand for all human beings in these writings) certainly prevails in the ways in which both the *Politics* and *Discourse on Method* theorise animals and animality, and they are often discussed alongside each other by contemporary animal theorists as evidence of the ways in which philosophy has historically dismissed nonhuman life. Reading these passages together gives the impression that everywhere in western thought we find animals divided from humans in a hierarchical arrangement. But there are important differences to take account of here. Rather than seeking to elevate humans to a transcendent sphere, Aristotle, biologist as much as philosopher, provides us with a materialist viewpoint on human life that focuses on vital functions that are shared, albeit expressed in different ways, with animals. This is clearly in evidence in his *History of Animals*, which attempts to account for a wide range of animal bodies and modes of life, and which stresses that animals have sensation and especially the experience of 'touch' (2005: 7). This emphasis on touch is something also outlined in his *De Anima*, which posits that far from being reduced to mere machines, animals have 'perceptive faculty' and 'desire' and can experience 'pain and pleasure' (1986: 162). What they don't have, however, is intellect or thought: sense-perception 'is enjoyed by all animals, while thinking admits of being false and is enjoyed by no animal that does not also have rationality' (197–8). Nonhuman animals have 'perceptive imagination' whereas humans have 'deliberative imagination' which depends on 'reasoning to decide whether to do one thing or another' (216). Significantly, Aristotle explains how animals, like humans but also plants, have souls: 'the soul is, so to speak, the first principle of living things'. His inquiry into the soul takes issue, then, with the privileged position of the human: 'at the moment those who talk or inquire about the soul seem to consider only the human case' (126–7). The soul for Aristotle is not, therefore, linked to either spirituality or personal identity; it is more like a 'vital principle' or 'principle of life' that fuels life from within the body (Thacker 2010: 11). The soul here is not a spiritual substance, as it is for Descartes, nor is it 'a guiding genius', as Plato conceptualised it, directing the body and lifting the human 'from earth towards our celestial affinity' (1965: 131). For Aristotle the soul remains firmly rooted to the earth: the animal is an 'ensouled *body*' (1986: 218).

Reflecting on the legacy of these philosophical conceptualisations of animals, Gilbert Simondon writes in *Two Lessons on Man and Animal* of how Aristotle offers a 'judgement on reality' which is 'the first objective naturalist doctrine of observation' (2011: 42–4). As such, Aristotle shows us that 'what occurs in man and what occurs in animals is comparable', signalling that they are neither identical nor entirely opposed (58). When Aristotle draws his own comparisons between humans and animals they consist of closely observed embodied realities. If we return to his *Politics*, we find one example from many where he discusses 'a number of different ways of life, among both animals and human beings':

> It is impossible to live without the means of subsistence; and among the animals we may notice that differences in the means of subsistence have produced consequent differences in ways of life. Some wild animals live in herds, and others are scattered in isolation, according as they find it convenient for the purpose of getting subsistence – some of them being carnivorous, some herbivorous, and some, again, omnivorous. Nature has thus distinguished their ways of life, with a view to their greater comfort and their better attainment of these things: indeed, as the same sort of food is not naturally agreeable to all members of a class, and as different sorts suit different species, there are also different ways of life even within the class of carnivorous animals – and equally in that of the herbivorous. The same is also true of men. Their ways of life differ considerably. (1995: 22)

Here the comparison is made between animals and humans not to draw a clear line of distinction, but to multiply differences in their respective modes of living – the emphasis falls on both *inter-* and *intra*-species difference. This diverges from the kind of comparisons we find throughout Descartes' *Discourse on Method*, which strikes a single line between humans as one category and animals as another. Descartes' teachings are, as Simondon bluntly puts it, 'quite frankly totally systematic and dichotomous doctrines . . . what is true of man is not at all true in regards to the animal' (2011: 59; 62). Cartesianism gives humans an alibi for their lack of concern for, or even cruelty towards, animals.

Souls and Sensations

The story of anthropocentrism differs not only between these two very different thinkers, but also within the wider contexts in which they are writing. While the most influential figures of their time, others from their periods have much to add to our thinking about animals today. Aristotle cannot stand for all antiquity's approach to animality any more than Plato can, as some voices were more firmly on the side of justice for animals among the ancient Greeks, taking issue with Aristotle's view that animals are naturally designed for utilisation by humans. For example, Pythagoras (c.570–c.495 BCE), Plutarch (c.46–c.120 CE) and Porphyry (c.234–c.305 CE) were important thinkers who promoted vegetarianism. Pythagoras' belief in the transmigration of souls from humans to animals meant that he objected on the grounds that humans could end up eating human souls, whereas Plutarch and Porphyry believed that animals were intelligent, sentient and even rational creatures who deserved moral consideration. Plutarch explicitly challenges the view that eating meat is 'natural to mankind' (2007: 156). Neither natural nor morally justifiable, 'the destruction of animals and the eating of flesh' for pleasure is, as Porphyry makes clear, 'savage and unjust' (1999: 41). Likewise, in the seventeenth century Descartes' worldview was met with challenges from other rationalist thinkers who couldn't agree with his viewpoint. Two significant figures in this respect are Baruch Spinoza and Gottfried Leibniz, both of whom challenged Cartesian mind-body dualism and the idea that matter was inert. Put simply, Spinoza and Leibniz offered a creative *monism* whereas Descartes offered a static *dualism*. Grounding human and nonhuman in an immanent – as opposed to transcendent – arrangement of life, they opened a space to think human and animal being in a non-oppositional, non-hierarchical manner.

That said, the most striking passage in Spinoza's writings in relation to animals appears to create precisely such a hierarchical opposition between humans and animals. Published in the year of his death in 1677, his *Ethics* contains the following extract which curiously echoes Descartes' dismissal of animal life:

> the law against killing animals is based more on empty superstition and unmanly compassion than sound reason. The rational principle of seeking our own advantage teaches us to establish a bond with men,

but not with the lower animals, or with things whose nature is different from human nature. We have the same right against them that they have against us. Indeed, because the right of each one is defined by his virtue, *or* power, men have a far greater right against the lower animals than they have against men. Not that I deny that the lower animals have sensations. But I do deny that we are therefore not permitted to consider our own advantage, use them at our pleasure, and treat them as is most convenient for us. For they do not agree in nature with us, and their affects are different in nature from human affects. (1996: 135)

In asserting the right of humans to kill animals and to utilise them for their own ends, Spinoza appears to hold different affects to be precisely what distinguishes humans from animals. But he doesn't deny that animals have sensations, nor, crucially, does he consistently set out to divide humans and animals in his writings. In fact, he rarely discusses animals explicitly in the *Ethics*, and in one other instance when he does he writes that 'many things are observed in the lower animals which far surpass human ingenuity' (72). The above passage is somewhat anomalous in the way it seems to draw a sharp difference in kind between animals 'whose nature is different from human nature'. As Hasana Sharp deftly argues, Spinoza's desire to distinguish here between human affects and animal affects is a result of his (admittedly anthropocentric) pragmatism in wanting to affirm connections between humans – he was concerned that sympathy for animals (which was growing in this period) would distract or undermine efforts to create bonds between humans. Spinoza's fear of the closeness between human and animal actually betrays an ontological acknowledgment of their closeness (Sharp 2011: 64). But the space opened by the *Ethics* to challenge human superiority and the human/animal boundary (a space that Cartesianism closes off) is what matters most. Where the effect of Descartes' dominance in the first half of that century was, as Gilles Deleuze writes in *Expressionism in Philosophy: Spinoza*, 'to devaluate Nature by taking away from it any virtuality or potentiality, any immanent power, any inherent being', Spinoza's fundamental role in the anti-Cartesian 'reaction' was aimed at 're-establishing the claims of a Nature endowed with forces of power' (1992: 228).

Leibniz is also part of this anti-Cartesian reaction, but he writes quite differently, and more extensively, about nonhuman animals. In his *Monadology*, published in 1714, he discusses their 'souls', 'heightened perceptions' and access to a 'memory' that 'resembles reason'. He turns to a dog to provide an example of an ability to call upon memories associated with particular items and events: 'animals which have a perception of something that strikes them and of which they have previously had a similar perception expect, from the representation in their memory, that which has been conjoined in that previous perception'. They are therefore 'led to sensations similar to those they have had before. For example, when one shows a stick to dogs, they recall the pain that it has caused them and whine and run off' (1991: 20). Leibniz goes on to describe how 'men function like beasts' (even specifying that they do so 'in three-quarters of [their] actions') in the ways that such perceptions and memories are connected. Men are not simply viewed as being the same as animals, then. The former have 'reason' and 'knowledge of ourselves and of God' – which Leibniz calls 'the rational soul or *spirit*' – and are therefore 'elect' animals 'elevated to the rank of reason and to the prerogative of spirits' (20; 28). But although there is a kind of hierarchy in Leibniz's system between animals with perception and sensation and humans with reason, it is not one that separates along clear, oppositional lines; in Leibniz's work we find a subtler differentiation. Despite interpretations of the *Monadology* which downplay the significance of animals, Glenn Hartz rightly points out that they have 'a fundamental, rigorous, serious status' in Leibniz's work. They are 'mind-independent – hence not "phenomena"' (Hartz 2006: 159). In contrast to a transcendent soul which divides human and nonhuman in Descartes, here the soul among humans and animals is, recalling Aristotle, in a 'harmonious' relation to the body (Leibniz 1991: 27). For Leibniz the 'simple substance of life' is expressed by both human and nonhuman creatures in an 'interlinkage or accommodation'; an animal, like a human, is 'a perpetual living mirror of the universe'; all matter, and therefore all souls, are 'interconnected' in a 'whole world of creatures'. The animal has not been elevated to join the human in a Cartesian transcendent sphere so much as the human has been de-transcendentalised so that it is, like the animal, conceived as a 'natural automaton' (24–6).

By the very end of the seventeenth and into the eighteenth century, philosophers other than Spinoza and Leibniz had offered profound challenges to Descartes' view of animals as mere automata. This is evident in the empiricism of John Locke and David Hume, who in different ways expose the limitations of human knowledge and reason and explicitly assign animals more lively capacities than modern philosophy hitherto allowed. In *An Essay Concerning Human Understanding*, published in 1690, Locke outlines capacities of sensation, perception and retention 'in some degree, in all sorts of animals' (2014: 138). Without wanting to equate the capacities of all animals, he is careful to emphasise the 'quickness and variety of sensation' in certain animals as well as those in whom 'the avenues provided by nature for the reception of sensations are so few, and the perception they are received with so obscure and dull'. No animal, however limited in sensory capacities it may seem (Locke gives the example of an oyster or cockle), can be reduced to 'perfect insensibility' (138–9). In a further example, Locke turns to birds as providing evidence of a nonhuman capacity for memory: 'birds learning of tunes, and the endeavors one may observe in them to hit the notes right, put it past doubt with me, that they have perception, and retain ideas in their memories, and use them for patterns' (144). Locke therefore recognises knowledge-gaining capacities in animals other than humans.

Hume's *An Enquiry Concerning Human Understanding*, published over half a century later in 1748, brings humans and animals into even closer contact by exposing the narrow bound of human understanding that is based on *a priori*, quasi-divine reasoning (2007: 5). Instead, Hume argues that knowledge, for both humans and animals, comes *from* the sensation of experience:

> animals, as well as men, learn many things from experience, and infer,
> that the same events will always follow from the same causes. By this
> principle they become acquainted with the more obvious properties
> of external objects, and gradually, from their birth, treasure up a
> knowledge of the nature of fire, water, earth, stones, heights, depths . . .
> and of the effects, which result from their operation. (76)

Moving away from easy oppositions that would confine animals to instinctive behaviour while humans enact learned behaviour, Hume recognises that through the experience of learning animals 'may be taught any course of action, the most contrary to their natural instincts and propensities'. In his view animals have foresight: 'the animal infers some fact beyond what immediately strikes his senses'. Disposing with oppositions between innate instinct and cultivated learning, then, Hume posits a kind of *learned instinct* based on experience 'which we possess in common with beasts, and on which the whole conduct of life depends'. This learned instinct replaces reason, which according to Hume governs neither human nor animal life (77–8).

In both Locke and Hume we find a simultaneous challenge to human mastery through an awareness of the limitations of human knowledge and an emphasis on the possibilities other animals have for knowledge. Taken together, the challenges to Cartesianism in the seventeenth and eighteenth centuries transform the terms of debate about human and nonhuman life. Instead of dividing humans from animals based on their transcendent capacities for thought, we must think about their relation in terms of material interconnections and embodied experiences. Neither Spinoza nor Leibniz, Locke nor Hume, simply *equate* humans and animals in their philosophy; rather, they open up pathways to challenge hierarchical and oppositional modes of thinking. However much Cartesian dualism would persist in western minds and discourse, these other philosophers complicate the legacy of Enlightenment thought on animality. When not consigned to merely mechanistic behaviour, animals become more lively and varied creatures.

ANIMAL STUDIES AND ANIMAL THEORY

Grappling with the complicated legacy of anthropocentric (and non-anthropocentric) philosophy, a diverse range of theoretical approaches to animals and animality have emerged since the Enlightenment and especially in the post-Darwinian age of the last 150 years. *Animal Theory* introduces, and critically engages with, some of the most influential and important of these: from the materialist ontology of Friedrich Nietzsche to the feminist philosophy of Donna Haraway; from the psychoanalytic theory of Sigmund Freud and Jacques Lacan to the moral philosophy of Peter Singer, Tom Regan and Martha Nussbaum; from the phenomenology of Martin Heidegger and Maurice Merleau-Ponty to the poststructuralist philosophy of Derrida, Deleuze and Félix Guattari; from the vegetarian theory of Carol Adams to the posthumanism of Cary Wolfe and Rosi Braidotti. To engage with these thinkers, who are often writing in very different contexts, is to open up a wide range of issues about the ways in which humans and animals imaginatively, ontologically and ethically relate to one another. By placing animals and animality at the centre of critical enquiry we can better understand, more rigorously conceptualise, and more fully account for the ways in which human and nonhuman life is entangled. The term 'animal theory' therefore points to two complementary aims of this project: to explore developments in the ways that post-Enlightenment philosophers conceptualise animals and animality; and to discuss the place of animals in current theoretical debates.

Animal Theory has a close relationship to the academic and activist work currently undertaken in the broader field of 'animal studies'. While the former is concerned explicitly with theoretical concepts, these are connected to wider material contexts often engaged with more fully by the latter. Developing rapidly over the past two decades, animal studies interrogates the exploitation of animals through the global agricultural industry, medical and cosmetic research, hunting, the destruction of natural habitats, domestication and the captivation of animals in zoos. The field itself is referred to variously as 'critical animal studies' (McCance 2013), 'human-animal studies' (Marvin and McHugh 2014), or 'animality studies' (Lundblad 2009), terms which respectively signal slightly different agendas: that animal studies is about critique; that it is always already about the relationship between humans and animals; or that it can provide space to analyse the history of representations of animality with a primary focus on human cultures. Whatever term we use, scholars working on questions relating to animals and animality share the aim of countering anthropocentrism by simultaneously critiquing human exceptionalism – the sense that we are a superior species – and more rigorously exploring the representation, lives and interests of animals which have at best been undervalued and at worst gone unnoticed. As Paul Waldau suggests in his recent introduction to the field, to address the marginalisation of animals requires 'the utmost in human humility about our abilities and limits, just as we need complete candor about our complicated heritages of compassion and oppression. We also need our most careful forms of thinking and the best of our soaring imagination' (2013: 1). This simultaneous emphasis on de-centring the human by using our distinctly human form of humility and imaginative thinking marks the paradoxical challenge facing those working in the field of animal studies, including those engaged in theoretical debates.

In order to meet the challenges of more carefully and rigorously exploring the relationship between human and nonhuman animals, animal studies has developed a fundamentally interdisciplinary ethos and scope. This is vibrantly on display in various journal special issues about animals that have been published in recent years. For example, the 2009 special issue of *PMLA* themed on 'Animal Studies' includes essays on literature, visual arts, zoos, feminism, queer studies, theatre and postcolonial studies, and this range is replicated in special issues of interdisciplinary journals such as *Hypatia* on 'Animal Others' (Gruen and Weil 2012), *New Formations* on 'The Animals Turn' (Wheeler and Williams 2012) and a double special issue of *Mosaic* on 'The Animal' (McCance 2006/7). Essays included in journals such as the *Journal for Critical Animal Studies, Society and Animals* and *Humanimalia* – all valuable resources for animal studies scholars – underscore this richness in scope, with essays ranging from philosophy to disability studies, from activism to religion, from criminology to the politics of museum exhibitions. But as well as bringing work from various disciplines into contact, animal studies also challenges the very core of what certain disciplines mean, the assumptions they have been based on, and what their goals are. In the 'humanities' disciplines, for example, researchers working on animals in subjects like literature, philosophy and history trouble what it means to be classified as a 'humanities' scholar in the first place – we are left to wonder what an 'animal humanities' or a 'posthumanities' would look like. This might explain why the term 'transdisciplinary' is now used with increasing frequency to define the kind of work animal studies scholars do. This term, as Wolfe has argued, is useful because it signals 'a kind of distributed reflexivity necessitated . . . by the fact that (by definition) *no* discourse, no discipline, can make transparent the conditions of its own observations' (2010: 116). The transdisciplinarity of animal studies is not just about transgressing disciplinary boundaries or showing a heightened awareness of the boundaries within which critics speak, but about reminding us that our disciplines don't straightforwardly reveal truths but offer partial, messy and impure methodologies, practices and theories for understanding life.

Theoretical approaches to animals speak not only to the transdisciplinary field of animal studies, but also to developments in contemporary theory more broadly. These approaches can be understood as part of a growing shift away from critical debates centred on questions of human culture, language and subjectivity and towards an explicit concern with nonhuman bodies, objects and environments. Yet in current theoretical discourse serious engagement with animal studies is still somewhat marginalised. A sample of recent books on the shifts in perspective in contemporary theory illustrates this: in Nicolas Birns' *Theory After Theory: An Intellectual History of Literary Theory from 1950 to the Early 21st Century*, there is one brief and incidental mention of animal studies, and one paragraph on Derrida's *The Animal That Therefore I Am* (2010: 164; 121); and in *Theory After 'Theory'*, edited by Jane Elliot and Derek Attridge, the cluster of three essays on 'Biopolitics and Ethics' are of interest to animal studies scholars, but none of them are directly concerned with theorising animality (2011: 179–220). One recent exception is Jean-Michel Rabaté's *Crimes of the Future: Theory and its Global Reproduction*, which contains a chapter on animals that discusses Derrida and Levinas among others (2014: 57–76). More generally, Rabaté's book offers an important reminder that what we call 'Theory' is intimately bound up with the history of philosophy which is 'the place where it was born': 'Theory should work through philosophy relentlessly, destabilizing it in the name of other discourses' (52). The dual task for animal theorists today is to destabilise the philosophical models of the past at the same time as forging alternative modes of thought. As *Animal Theory* attempts to demonstrate, new theoretical approaches to animals depend not on a clean break with all western philosophical discourses but on a reassessment of their epistemological, ontological and ethical claims.

There is a final point about terminology that is significant in thinking about animal theory and its relationship to animal studies, which involves how we refer to the object of enquiry. The wide and frequent use of the term 'animal' has been criticised for erasing the multiplicity of animals by reducing singular beings to the 'animal in general'. 'The animal', Derrida reminds us, 'is a word, it is an appellation that men have instituted, a name they have given themselves the right and the authority to give the living other' (2008: 30; 23). Additionally, the use of the term 'nonhuman' is also 'ideologically loaded' because, as Marianne DeKoven points out, it categorises the animal as the negative of the human: 'only from the point of view of the human are other animals nonhuman' (2009: 363). As she goes on to suggest: '*Nonhuman* is not an inevitable descriptor. There are many other ways to designate the beings in question: by species, habitat, ecological niche, relation to predation (predator or prey), type of nourishment (carnivore, herbivore, omnivore). *Non-white*, *non-European*, and *non-Western* are parallel to *nonhuman* and reveal what is at stake in using it' (363). The 'nonhuman' 'animal' therefore engages terms that need to be worked though, critiqued and perhaps, eventually, disposed of. Where possible this book refers to the plural 'animals' as the preferred alternative (though this word is not without its own limitations in that it still works as a catch-all for a heterogeneous array of creatures), but there are times when it is necessary to refer to the 'nonhuman' and/or 'animal' in order to draw attention to the ways such terms have figured in theoretical discourse, and to expose their limitations. It is hoped that in reading *Animal Theory* the critical tools will be provided to interrogate not just these words but also a range of other all-too-familiar terms explored in this book such as 'meaning', 'being', 'thinking', 'language', 'subjectivity', 'agency', 'world' and, not least, 'human'.

CHAPTER OVERVIEW

The chapters of this book are designed to introduce readers to a broad history of approaches to theorising animals in modern and contemporary philosophy and to connect these writings to current theoretical debates. Any book of this nature will inevitably afford more attention and analysis to certain thinkers at the expense of others, and cannot be exhaustive in its scope. But the range of texts, contexts and concepts covered have been selected so as to provide a firm grounding in the key issues at stake in theorising animals and to raise a range of questions for discussion. The book is therefore written in such a way that it will offer something to readers new to the theoretical material but will also consolidate knowledge and open up new directions in thought to those who are more familiar with the issues under discussion. The chapters have been set out so as to broadly follow a trajectory from a focus on human concerns to animal concerns (though, as will become clear, these are frequently inter-related): from a consideration of the ways in which animals are thought of as human substitutes (Chapter 1), to a discussion of human animality (Chapter 2), an exploration of the everyday lives and worlds of animals (Chapter 3), and finally an analysis of ethical responses to animals (Chapter 4). The intention is not to suggest a straightforward, linear progression towards placing the animal at the centre of theoretical inquiry, but rather to approach, from different angles, modes of non-anthropocentric thought which have emerged concurrently with thinking that continues to be centred on the human. Additional features have been added to complement the theoretical discussion. Most notably, each chapter closes with close readings of contemporary literary texts which explore themes engaged with in the chapter but also point towards issues relevant to the reading of animals in literature more generally. As well as focusing on literary devices and narrative techniques, these texts have been chosen to represent a range of forms (a short story by Angela Carter, a creative essay by J. M. Coetzee, a novel by Paul Auster, and a work of non-fiction by Jonathan Safran Foer), and to show how literary texts themselves theorise animals and animality. Given the often close relationship between those interested in animal theory and in literary studies, it is hoped these sections will offer further examples of how our thinking about animals is linked to our reading of animals, whether in literary or theoretical texts. Finally, at the end of each chapter a list of 'Key Texts' contains the bibliographical information for the primary material covered, and a list of 'Further Reading' contains bibliographical information for secondary sources referred to in the chapters alongside some additional recommended material.

One of the first major challenges when thinking about animals is precisely to think about them *as animals*. Chapter 1, 'Animals as Humans', explores the ways in which theoretical writings about animals often transform them into symbols and metaphors to explain primarily human concerns. It turns firstly to psychoanalytic theory, and in particular the work of Freud and Lacan. Animals feature prominently in Freud's analysis of the development of civilisation from primitive societies to post-Darwinian modernity, as well as in his interpretations of dreams and phobias. Likewise, studies of animal behaviour are often used in Lacan's writings on subject-formation. However, their interest in animality is often undermined by the use of animal figures as substitutes for human fears and desires, or as points of contrast for an exploration of human language. The second part of the chapter goes on to consider the relative pitfalls and potential of 'anthropomorphism' as the process of attributing human qualities to nonhuman life. This includes a discussion of Thomas Nagel's engagement with the question of how possible it is for a human to imagine what it is like to be an animal, and an analysis of recent attempts to detach anthropomorphism from anthropocentrism. Given the prevalence of anthropomorphism in literary texts as well as in theoretical works, the chapter closes with a reading of Carter's 'Lizzie's Tiger', which offers nuanced strategies for representing animality.

Where the first chapter demonstrates the ways in which thinking about animals can lead to their appropriation as vehicles to convey human concerns, Chapter 2 turns its attention to thinking about *humans* as animals. 'Animal Ontology' examines modes of being human and animal both in themselves and in their relationality. Focusing on key works by Nietzsche, Deleuze and Guattari and Haraway, it investigates how a recognition of the shared animality of both the human and nonhuman can transform ontological boundaries that seek to hierarchically divide beings along lines of nature and culture. These thinkers provide concepts – whether Nietzsche's 'Superman', Deleuze and Guattari's 'becoming-animal', or Haraway's 'becoming-with' – that engage with animality in order to affirm a materialist and immanent understanding of life. The chapter then goes on to assess the relationship between animal theory, posthumanism, new materialism and contemporary neo-Marxist philosophy in an effort to consider the political import that an ontology founded on non/human entanglements may have. As this chapter takes seriously the animality of both human and nonhuman animals, the concluding section details what is at stake in reading animals literally rather than metaphorically by turning to Coetzee's book *The Lives of Animals*.

Having affirmed the animality of the human, and delineated an intimate relation between human being and animal being, Chapter 3 is explicitly concerned with 'Animal Life'. It begins with a discussion of domesticated animals, and the pets who have in different ways inspired the work of Derrida, Haraway and Vicki Hearne. Focusing on Derrida's bathroom encounter with his cat alongside Haraway's and Hearne's accounts of dog training, it considers the extent to which living with animals allows us to think with them. The chapter then turns to phenomenological inquiries into animality by unpacking Heidegger's thesis of the animal as 'poor-in-world' and Merleau-Ponty's conceptualisation of animals as part of 'the flesh of the world'. At stake in these phenomenological approaches to animal life is the attempt to understand how animals experience their environments, and how this relates to the ways in which humans make sense of the world. The chapter concludes with an analysis of Auster's attempt to write the life of a dog in *Timbuktu*, a task that is especially difficult given the canine reliance on smell over speech in experiencing the world.

While understanding how humans relate to animals in daily life is vitally important, the stark reality of animal suffering and exploitation means that humans frequently encounter animals once these animals have, for various reasons, been killed. Chapter 4, 'Animal Ethics', charts the ways in which the lives and deaths of animals enter human moral consideration. The first part of the chapter documents three of the most significant developments in ethical approaches to animals: Singer's 'utilitarianism', Regan's theory of 'animal rights', and Nussbaum's 'capabilities' approach. While all three pay serious attention to animals and have done much to affect the ways in which they are treated, they have various differences and limitations. Moving beyond utilitarian and rights-based frameworks, the chapter then goes on to examine how useful notions of 'fellowship' and 'recognisability' are in animal ethics by engaging with Cora Diamond, Derrida and Emmanuel Levinas. Finally, the chapter turns to perhaps the most pressing ethical issue concerning animals today: the production and consumption of meat. It considers vegetarianism and the sexual, racial and cultural politics of eating animals with reference to Carol Adams and Marjorie Spiegel alongside Derrida and Haraway. In many ways, such thinkers base their theorising in a mode of story-telling, and the chapter, and book, concludes with a discussion of the relationship between eating and story-telling in Foer's *Eating Animals*.

Engaging with theoretical approaches to animals and animality may not provide us with the embodied creaturely encounters that take place in zoos, but they do help us to think more carefully about what it actually means to be 'human' or 'animal', and the epistemological, ontological and ethical assumptions that are between these (often disappointing) encounters. By introducing and intervening in critical debates in animal theory, it is hoped that this book will provide an opening to think and read differently as the thinking and reading animals that we are. Rather than distancing us from our embodied and emotional relationship to other animals, thinking and reading *as* animals enacts a more responsive, generous and humble mode of living as one species among – not above – many.

KEY TEXTS

Aristotle (1986), *De Anima (On the Soul)*, trans. Hugh Lawson-Tancred, London: Penguin.

Aristotle (1995), *Politics*, trans. Ernest Barker, Oxford: Oxford University Press.

Berger, John (2009), *Why Look at Animals?*, London: Penguin.

Descartes, René (1968), *Discourse on Method* and *The Meditations*, trans. F. E. Sutcliffe, London: Penguin.

Hume, David (2007), *An Enquiry Concerning Human Understanding*, Oxford: Oxford University Press.

Leibniz, G. W. (1991), *Monadology: An Edition for Students*, ed. Nicholas Rescher, London: Routledge.

Locke, John (2014), *An Essay Concerning Human Understanding*, Hertfordshire: Wordsworth.

Simondon, Gilbert (2011), *Two Lessons on Man and Animal*, trans. Drew S. Burk, Minneapolis: Univocal.

Spinoza, Benedict de (1996), *Ethics*, trans. Edwin Curley, London: Penguin.

FURTHER READING

Aristotle (2005), *History of Animals*, trans. Richard Cresswell, Elibron.

Baratay, Eric and Elisabeth Hardouin-Fugier (2003), *Zoo: A History of Zoological Gardens in the West*, London: Reaktion.

Birns, Nicholas (2010), *Theory After Theory: An Intellectual History of Literary Theory from 1950 to the Early 21st Century*, Peterborough: Broadview.

DeKoven, Marianne (2009), 'Why Animals Now?', *PMLA* 124.2, 361–9.

Deleuze, Gilles (1992), *Expressionism in Philosophy: Spinoza*, trans. Martin Joughin, New York: Zone Books.

DeMello, Margo (2012), *Animals and Society: An Introduction to Human-Animal Studies*, New York: Columbia University Press.

Derrida, Jacques (2008), *The Animal That Therefore I Am*, trans. David Wills, New York: Fordham University Press.

Derrida, Jacques (2009), *The Beast and the Sovereign*, vol. 1, trans. Geoffrey Bennington, Chicago: University of Chicago Press.

Elliott, Jane and Derek Attridge (eds) (2011), *Theory After 'Theory'*, London: Routledge.

Gruen, Lori and Kari Weil (eds) (2012), 'Special Issue: Animal Others', *Hypatia: A Journal of Feminist Philosophy*, 27.3.

Ham, Jennifer and Matthew Senior (eds) (1997), *Animal Acts: Configuring the Human in Western History*, New York: Routledge.

Hartz, Glenn (2006), *Leibniz's Final System: Monads, Matter and Animals*, New York: Routledge.

Jamieson, Dale (2006), 'Against Zoos', in Peter Singer (ed.), *In Defense of Animals: The Second Wave*, Oxford: Blackwell, pp. 132–43.

Lundblad, Michael (2009), 'From Animal to Animality Studies', *PMLA* 124.2, 496–502.

McCance, Dawne (ed.) (2006/7), 'Special Issue: The Animal', *Mosaic* 39.4/40.1.

McCance, Dawne (2013), *Critical Animal Studies: An Introduction*, Albany: State University of New York Press.

McHugh, Susan (2011), *Animal Stories: Narrating Across Species Lines*, Minneapolis: University of Minnesota Press.

Marvin, Garry and Susan McHugh (2014), *Routledge Handbook of Human-Animal Studies*, London: Routledge.

Mullan, Bob and Garry Marvin (1999), *Zoo Culture*, Second Edition, Urbana and Chicago: University of Illinois Press.

Plato (1965), *Timaeus*, ed. and trans. John Warrington, New York: Everyman's.

Plutarch (2007), 'The Eating of Flesh', in Linda Kalof and Amy Fitzgerald (eds), *The Animals Reader: The Essential Classic and Contemporary Writings*, Oxford: Berg, pp. 154–7.

Porphyry (1999), 'On Abstinence from Animal Food', in Kerry S. Walters and Lisa Portmess (eds), *Ethical Vegetarianism: From Pythagoras to Peter Singer*, Albany: State University of New York Press, pp. 35–46.

Rabaté, Jean-Michel (2014), *Crimes of the Future: Theory and its Global Reproduction*, New York: Bloomsbury.

Ritvo, Harriet (1987), 'Exotic Captives', in *The Animal Estate: The English and Other Creatures in the Victorian Age*, Cambridge MA: Harvard University Press, pp. 205–42.

Rothfels, Nigel (2002), *Savages and Beasts: The Birth of the Modern Zoo*, Baltimore: Johns Hopkins University Press.

Rousseau, Jean-Jacques (2009), *Discourse on the Origin of Inequality*, trans. Franklin Philip, Oxford: Oxford University Press.

Senior, Matthew (ed.) (2007), *A Cultural History of Animals in the Age of Enlightenment*, New York: Berg.

Sharp, Hasana (2011), 'Animal Affects: Spinoza and the Frontiers of the Human', *Journal for Critical Animal Studies* IX. 1/2, 48–68.

Thacker, Eugene (2010), *After Life*, Chicago: University of Chicago Press.

Vaughan, Adam (2014), 'London Zoo Under Investigation After Beer Thrown Over Tiger', *Guardian*, 31 July 2014; at <http://www.theguardian.com/environment/2014/jul/31/london-zoo-beer-tiger-westminster-council-investigation> (accessed 15 December 2014).

Waldau, Paul (2013), *Animal Studies: An Introduction*, Oxford: Oxford University Press.

Weil, Kari (2012), *Thinking Animals: Why Animal Studies Now?* New York: Columbia University Press.

Wheeler, Wendy and Linda Williams (eds) (2012), 'Special Issue: The Animals Turn', *New Formations* 76.

Wolfe, Cary (2010), '"Animal Studies", Disciplinarity, and the (Post) Humanities', in *What is Posthumanism?*, Minneapolis: University of Minnesota Press, pp. 99–126.

CHAPTER I

Animals as Humans

[handwritten: If, How does does Dots Dos poems questian Heirarchy?]

PSYCHOANALYTIC ANIMALS

When hierarchical divides are constructed between humans and animals they are frequently based both on undervaluing animal life and inflating the significance of humanity. Psychoanalytic theory is important to animal theory because it occupies a complicated position in relation to these two attitudes. On the one hand it was seen by Sigmund Freud to provide the third great strike against 'the universal narcissism of men'. The two previous blows were struck in the 'cosmological' and 'biological' realms: firstly, the Copernican revolution, which in the sixteenth century revealed that the earth, and therefore 'mankind', could no longer be thought of as the centre of the universe; and secondly, Darwin's theory of evolution, which in the nineteenth century presented the shared origins of species, showing that 'man is not a being different from animals or superior to them'. Freud's third 'psychological' development claims that while 'man feels himself to be supreme within his own mind', this mind is in fact 'a labyrinth of impulses' that are rooted in 'unconscious mental processes' (Freud 2001: 139–43). But, on the other hand, psychoanalysis as a field of study can be critiqued for using animals as symbolical and metaphorical devices to reveal truths about the human psyche, whether this relates to de-centring human subjectivity, interpreting dreams or accessing language. To assess the treatment of animals in psychoanalytic theory therefore reveals the difficulties that result from thinking about animals *as humans* – that is to say, when we as humans think about animals with an interest primarily in humanity, but also when we think of animals as themselves human substitutes or stand-ins.

[handwritten: How are they substitutes?]

De-centring Human Subjectivity

In claiming that '*the ego is not master in its own house*' (Freud 2001: 143), psychoanalytic theory radically de-centres the human subject. This is a key feature of Freud's 1930 study *Civilization and Its Discontents*, where he describes the belief in a stable 'sense of self' fuelled by an 'autonomous, uniform' ego as 'a delusion'; psychoanalytic theory instead tells us that 'the ego extends inwards, with no clear boundary, into an unconscious psychical entity that we call the id, and for which it serves, so to speak, as a façade' (2004: 3). By judging the ego – the seat of what distinguishes so-called 'civilised' humans – to be connected with unconscious psychical structures, Freud in turn asserts the link between the civilised and primitive. There is some 'retention of the primitive' in even the most civilised of humans (by whom Freud invariably means white western European men) (6). Primitive man is, as he puts it in his earlier 1913 book *Totem and Taboo*, 'still our contemporary. There are men still living who, as we believe, stand very near to primitive man, far nearer than we do, and whom we therefore regard as his direct heirs and representatives' (1960: 1).

The significance of the context in which Freud is writing, in the sense that he sees it as the culmination of a long historical process of de-centring the human, is emphasised in both of these texts. While it is helpful, as mentioned above, to situate his writings in relation to Copernicus and Darwin, in *Totem and Taboo* Freud offers an even broader context in which to understand this de-centring of humanity. He outlines three systems of thought, what he calls 'three great pictures of the universe': namely the 'animistic (or mythological)', the 'religious' and the 'scientific' (77). In the animistic phase, where spiritual agencies are assigned to animals and the natural world more widely, humans 'ascribe omnipotence to *themselves*'. At the religious phase 'they transfer it to the gods', but in doing so they 'reserve the power of influencing the gods in a variety of ways according to their wishes'. The third, and ongoing, scientific phase, however, 'no longer affords any room for human omnipotence; men have acknowledged their smallness', even though 'the primitive belief' in human mastery persists to some extent and creates the illusion of human power (88). According to this sweeping historical trend, humans have moved from being the most significant to relatively insignificant beings. But this scientific phase has yet to be matched by an acceptance that humans are not the pinnacle and centre of life (we might think here of the ways in which Darwinian theory has inadvertently led many to see evolution as evidence of man's more developed nature). In one sense, Freud's own writing works to expose the 'arrogance which urges adult civilized men to draw a hard-and-fast line between their own nature and that of all other animals' (126–7).

In charting this progression towards a de-centred human subject, however, Freud is clearly still offering a human-centred analysis of history. Rather than seeking to detail the lives, behaviours and environments of nonhuman animals, Freud is primarily concerned with exploring the flawed ways in which the human subject has been privileged and the arrogance which assumes that humans are perfected beings. At times this results in him offering a critique of civilisation without fully turning his back on many of the models, assumptions and achievements of it. In one sense, then, *Civilization and Its Discontents* is about the limitations of human world-making capacities – the 'delusional reshaping of reality'– and the 'superior power of nature' (Freud 2004: 23; 29). Freud takes care not to agree 'with the prejudice that civilization is synonymous with a trend towards perfection' that is 'pre-ordained for mankind' (43). But at the same time Freud's view that humanity has nonetheless managed to 'increase its control over nature' through 'extraordinary advances' in science means that we shouldn't have 'hostility to civilization' or see civilisation as an 'enemy' (30–1; 60). He therefore claims an 'impartiality' which allows him to both consider criticisms of the aims of civilisation 'without bridling' and 'refrain from the enthusiastic prejudice that sees our civilization as the most precious thing we possess or can acquire' (105). This concession could itself be seen as a kind of de-centring of the ego, even if it appears in a study that is very clearly centred on examining human civilisation.

The extent to which Freud's analysis in *Civilization and Its Discontents* takes as its central concern the civilised human subject is evident in those passages which do refer directly to animals. As can be seen from Aristotle to Descartes, animals have traditionally been used to define a split with civilised (for Aristotle read 'political' and for Descartes read 'thinking') beings, and Freud appears to engage that tradition: civilisation 'designates the sum total of those achievements and institutions that distinguish our life from that of our animal ancestors and serve the dual purpose of protecting human beings against nature and regulating their mutual relations' (34). What is striking here is the way in which civilisation is a generalised, trans-historical category that is set against the 'animal' as itself one homogeneous life form rooted to 'nature'. Tantalisingly, elsewhere Freud suggests that what is meant by the term 'animal' is in need of serious discussion. When arguing that it is wrong-headed to focus on any 'purpose' of life, he notes: 'No one talks about the purpose of the life of animals, unless it is that they are meant to serve human beings.' And yet, he adds, the possibility of doing so is 'untenable, for there are many animals that man can do nothing with – except describe, classify and study them – and countless animal species have escaped even this use by living and dying out before man set eyes on them' (15). Freud acknowledges that the experiences of many animals evade human capture and control, but perhaps too quickly closes down specific questions about the lives of animals as a result.

Later in *Civilization and Its Discontents*, when focusing on humanity's 'struggle for existence', Freud turns again to animals. If, as he argues, human civilisation is marked by a struggle between the 'life drive', which caters for survival, pleasure and reproduction, and the 'death drive', which is an originary 'tendency to aggression' that 'represents the greatest obstacle to civilization' (74), then 'why', he asks, 'do our relatives, the animals, show no sign of such cultural struggle?' His response again posits human epistemological limitations:

> We have no way of knowing. It is very likely that some of them – the
> bees, the ants, the termites – struggled for thousands of centuries
> until they evolved the state institutions, the distribution of functions,
> the restrictions on individuals, for which we admire them today. It
> is characteristic of our present condition that we feel we should not
> be happy in any of these animal states or the roles assigned in them
> to individuals. In the case of other animal species it may be that a
> temporary compromise was reached between the influences of their
> surroundings and the conflicting drives within them, so that any
> development was brought to a halt . . . There are many questions to be
> asked, and as yet no answers. (76)

In this passage Freud appears to align animals in their present state to a fixed nature (as opposed to humans who have a still developing culture). Animal life is suspended on two levels: firstly, in the curious speculation that animal evolution has now halted; secondly, in the unwillingness (couched as inability) to expand on these speculations about zoological life in more detail. In highlighting how animals are rarely considered by humans other than for their instrumental value, the irony is that Freud himself never attempts to answer these questions about different species. Once again, this can be seen as a sign of epistemological modesty (and a reluctance to bring animals into human frameworks of thought in order to avoid equating animal life with human life), but it can also be viewed as an unwillingness to radically challenge certain anthropocentric epistemological boundaries.

Dreams and Phobias

Animals figure prominently in Freud's case studies of dreams, where he developed his psychoanalytic interpretations before turning this methodology onto the wider questions of culture and civilisation in texts such as *Totem and Taboo* and *Civilization and Its Discontents*. In an often-cited passage from *The Interpretation of Dreams*, first published in 1900, he remarks: 'What animals dream of I do not know. A proverb for which I am indebted to one of my pupils professes to tell us, for it asks the question: "What does the goose dream of?" and answers: "Of maize." The whole theory that the dream is the fulfil-ment of a wish is contained in these two sentences' (1997: 43). A comparison is drawn here between humans and animals in terms of 'wish-fulfilment', where all dreams are seen as playing out desires. Rather than serious specula-tion about the dreams of geese, or any other animals, Freud's concern is with the way these animals become part of a system of wish-fulfilment revealed in human dreams. Humans, it is implied, don't dream directly of the object desired the way geese dream of maize. This is because human dreams have both 'manifest' and 'latent' content, where the manifest dream-content is the material produced by the dream or the literal rendering of the dream, and the latent dream-thought is the meaning buried underneath or the unconscious desires coded in a system of symbols (46). Animal dreams are assumed to be based solely on manifest dream-content, whereas deciphering human dreams requires more sophisticated interpretive strategies: 'The dream-content is, as it were, presented in hieroglyphics, whose symbols must be translated, one by one, into the language of the dream-thoughts.' Instead of reading such symbols 'in accordance with their values as pictures' we should consider them 'in accordance with their meaning as symbols' (169–70). Dreams have a 'secret meaning'; their 'riddles and contradictions' must be 'solved' only through careful interpretation (50; 70).

In Freud's discussions of specific dreams, animals frequently play a key role in his attempts to make sense of the riddle of symbols. Where in other texts Freud admits failings in human understanding about the experiences of actual animals, he is much more comfortable dealing with animals in the abstract, once they have been transformed into figurative devices. In *The Interpretation of Dreams* this is most evident when animals become substitutes for the father, whether it is a lion's mane that represents a father's beard, or 'vicious animals, dogs, wild horses' that represent 'the dreaded father' (312; 270). Because Freudian psychoanalytic theory proposes that fear of emasculation at the hands of the father – what becomes known as 'castration anxiety' – results in regulation of sexual desire, the 'wild beasts serve to represent the *libido*, feared by the ego, and combated by repression' (270). This substitution of the animal for the father leads to animal phobias, as described in *Totem and Taboo*:

> a strange rift occurs in the excellent relations between children and animals. A child will suddenly begin to be frightened of some particular species of animal and to avoid touching or seeing any individual of that species. The clinical picture of an animal phobia emerges – a very common, and perhaps the earliest, form of psycho-neurotic illness occurring in childhood. As a rule the phobia is attached to animals in which the child has hitherto shown a specially lively interest and it has nothing to do with any particular individual animal. There is no large

choice of animals that may become objects of a phobia in the case of children living in towns: horses, dogs, cats, less often birds, and with striking frequency very small creatures such as beetles and butterflies. The senseless and immoderate fear shown in these phobias is sometimes attached to animals only known to the child from picture books and fairy tales. (1960: 127)

Whether encountered in towns or in picture books, such animal phobias have little to do with the chosen species and have 'nothing to do with any particular individual animal'. Freud found that 'when the children concerned were boys, their fear related at bottom to their father and had merely been displaced on to the animal' (127–8). These animals serve to allow the child to displace his ambivalent feelings towards his father. Moreover, such phobias combine Freud's concern with patriarchal structures on a socio-historical as well as a familial level, connecting his account of primitive laws or taboos to the regulation of desire struggled with through the Oedipus complex. Consider both of the principles that are the foundation of totemism (where an animal is selected as spiritual guardian of a clan): namely, that the totem shouldn't be killed and that it is forbidden for men to have sex with women who share the same totem. These two principles correspond to the two Oedipal 'primal wishes of children': the desire to kill the father and to create a union with the mother (132). According to Freud, the substitution of animals for fathers has been at the centre of the formation of sexual and social norms since the beginnings of civilisation.

If we look more closely at an instance of how animals enter the Oedipal dynamics of childhood development, we might say that, just as totem animals were sometimes sacrificed in the name of civilisation (133–4), so too on a psychosexual level animals are 'sacrificed' within a symbolic realm of human dreams. The 1909 case of five-year-old 'Little Hans' and his horse phobia poses a number of difficulties concerning psychoanalytic treatments of animals. Corresponding with Hans' father, who began analysing his son's behaviour when he was only three years old, Freud very quickly focuses on the role of animals as substitutes for the father. Commenting on an early episode when Hans stands in front of a lion's cage and calls out that he 'saw the lion's widdler', Freud interprets:

Animals owe a good deal of their importance in myths and fairy tales to the openness with which they display their genitals and their sexual functions to the inquisitive little human child. There can be no doubt about Hans' sexual curiosity; but it also roused the spirit of enquiry in him and enabled him to arrive at genuine abstract knowledge. (1977: 172–3)

The animal encounter leads to an abstracting of animality, and the knowledge gained is about the structure of what is present and what is absent. The child's reflections were judged to be as follows: '"A dog and a horse have widdlers; a table and a chair haven't." He had thus got hold of an essential characteristic for differentiating between animate and inanimate objects.' This discovery transfers onto the distinction between male and female sexes. Hans on seeing his mother replies: '"I thought you were so big you'd have a widdler like a horse"' (172–3). Hans' father reports that his son then develops a 'nervous disorder' whereby he is 'afraid *a horse will bite him in the street*' (185).

Hans' fear, according to his father, 'seems somehow to be connected with his having been frightened by a large penis'. But for Freud this explanation is too literal and straightforward. Instead, his analysis of the case corrects, or rather nuances, the father's explanation: 'It is true', writes Freud, 'that he was afraid of big animals because he was obliged to think of their big widdlers; but it cannot really be said that he was afraid of big widdlers themselves' (196–7). Instead, these large penises serve to remind Hans in the first instance of his own much smaller penis and, more significantly, this then mixes with the information that some people (i.e. women) don't have 'widdlers' at all: 'The piece of enlightenment which Hans had been given a short time before to the effect that women really do not possess a widdler was bound to have had a shattering effect upon his self-confidence and to have aroused his castration complex' (198). For Freud, what Hans really feared was the loss of his own penis, and the seat of the fear wasn't the horse but his father (who *is* the horse – Freud makes much of the fact that Hans mentions that he was 'particularly bothered by what horses wear in front of their eyes and by the black round their mouths', which he interprets to be the father's glasses and moustache). The horse's penis is transformed into a site of Oedipal drama, as Hans fears that his penis will be removed by his father because of his fondness for his mother. Animals such as horses, which surrounded Hans' everyday life, are not of much significance for their equine characteristics, but rather for what they stand-in for: the father, and the Oedipal schema, as regulator of desire. Freud may concede that psychoanalysis is not an exact science, and so we have to 'guess many things' (1977: 197), but such guesswork – the interpretative method Freud employs in the Little Hans case as elsewhere – has a tendency to lead to animals becoming substitutes for something other than themselves.

This can be charged of those psychoanalysts influenced by Freud, too. For example, in Melanie Klein's *Narrative of a Child Analysis*, we find that 'a cornucopia of imagery – animal, vegetable, and mineral – is so remorselessly reduced to the stark geometry of the Oedipal triangle' (Ellmann 2014: 337). Klein records ninety-three sessions over a four-month period with Richard, a ten-year-old boy who was judged to have a range of problems including the fact he was scared of other children and didn't want to leave the house – issues heightened by the onset of the Second World War in 1939. Of special interest in relation to Freud's case study of Little Hans' phobia is the eighth session, when a horse's head makes a significant appearance. Rather than appearing in a dream, this horse is simply observed by Richard from the window of the analyst's room. Having told Klein about how he 'had nearly bumped into a boy at the corner of the road' who 'looked very unfriendly', Richard shows her 'a horse's head at the turning of the road. (A horse and cart were standing there but the horse's body was hidden.) Richard looked again and again at the horse's head and seemed frightened of it' (Klein 1984: 44). Following this Richard turns to a map on the wall of the room: 'How very small Portugal was. He again looked at the map upside-down. He would like the shape of Europe if Turkey and Russia were not there. They seemed so "out of place"; they "bulged out" and were too big.' Klein, as we might expect, interprets 'the bulging Turkey, the horse's head at the turn of the road, and the hostile boy whom he also met at a corner, as standing for Daddy's frightening big genital inside Mummy'. 'In that way', she adds, 'Daddy was dangerous to Mummy in sexual relations; he was attacking her' (44). The horse is immediately equated with Richard's geopolitical comments and the close encounter with the boy, and is translated into a psychosexual familial drama where Richard is judged to 'wish to destroy Daddy because of fear as well as jealousy' (46). The session concludes with a comment about the horse which seemingly vindicates Klein's interpretive schema: after her 'interpretation about the horse's head at the corner, he looked in that direction again, said that the cart had moved, the horse was nearer, and its head looked quite nice'. For Klein this could never be a real feeling of affection for the horse, rather it is evidence of 'diminution of anxiety' and the success of the psychoanalytic method (47). Despite Klein's claims in her introduction that she always tried to avoid 'introducing any similes, metaphors', her whole interpretative strategy is indeed a metaphorical one. For Freud and Klein alike, anything that isn't literally mother and father must figuratively be so.

It is this figurative transformation or appropriation of the animal which is heavily criticised by Gilles Deleuze. In 'The Interpretation of Utterances', a 1977 polemical essay he, alongside his long-time collaborator Félix Guattari and his students at the time Claire Parnet and André Scala, offers an alternative reading of Freud's Little Hans and Klein's Richard. Following the expansive critique of psychoanalysis seen in Deleuze and Guattari's *Anti-Oedipus*, first published in French in 1972, they argue that in Freud's interpretation Hans is 'inoculated with the Oedipus virus' (Deleuze et al. 2007: 91). In the case of Little Hans they are scathing of the view that 'the horse must represent something else'; like other animals 'the response will always be the same: horse or giraffe, rooster or elephant, it's always papa' (96). Failing to consider other significant ways boy and horse could interact, Freud instead 'proceeds through static analogies of representations'. In a rhetorical flourish they turn the diagnosis onto the analyst: 'Who is sick? Little Hans? Or his father and the "professor" together? Ravaged by *interpretosis* and meaning' (97). The horse only exists on a symbolic level for Freud, and it is integrated into a schema that is pre-determined; it is an archetypical example of dogmatically *applying* a theoretical framework onto the world. According to the analysis of Deleuze and his collaborators, Freud fails to look at material and meaningful configurations in which the horse and the child are connected:

> A horse is an element, a specific material in a street-horse-omnibus-load assemblage. A horse, as we have seen, is defined by a list of affects depending on the assemblage into which it enters. These affects represent nothing other than themselves: being blinded, having a bit, being proud, having a big pee-maker, large haunches for making dung, biting, pulling over-sized loads, being whipped, falling, making a hullabaloo with its legs. (97)

Only by considering the significance of the horse's bodily affects can it be put *into action* rather than rendering it a passive and static symbol. In this alternative viewpoint, Hans' horse phobia isn't the result of 'an Oedipal fantasy' so much as a sign of his family's dominant control over him that doesn't allow him out into the street; the family's actions have created this fear in him rather than a universal and innate Oedipal fantasy having done so (98–100). Where Klein's Richard is concerned, 'The Interpretation of Utterances' reaches a similar conclusion: Richard's knowledge and feelings about childhood, politics, war and empire – and the animals that are entangled them – are quickly translated into 'fantasies' and reduced to the familial triangle. While based on the exchange of words between child and analyst, the aim of such psychoanalysis is in fact 'to prevent him from forming utterances' (103). The whole case demonstrates 'the shame of psychoanalysis' (101).

It is important not to be carried away by the rhetorical force of polemical critiques and simply dismiss psychoanalysis as altogether unimportant for animal theory. Recognising the significance of animals in the origins of psychoanalytic theory has the potential to uncover the complicated ways in which animals become associated with conscious and unconscious experience, and the crucial role that animal figures play in childhood development. Following animal figures as they appear in psychoanalytic theory is additionally an important task for animal theorists given that, as Nicholas Ray has recently commented, 'the so-called "question of the animal" still has a relatively limited circulation within psychoanalysis and psychoanalytic studies', with the relationship between humans and animals yet to come under the careful scrutiny that the wealth of appearances of animals in various theoretical texts and records of clinical cases demands (2012: 41; 2014). And yet, in beginning this work of following psychoanalytic animals, pointed critiques such as Deleuze's demonstrate that what is often at stake is the question of how *anthropocentrism* meets *anthropomorphism*; that is, how a human-centred analysis depends upon ascribing nonhuman animals with human features or forms. 'Anthropomorphism' is precisely the word used in 'The Interpretation of Utterances' to explain how 'Freud does not understand animals' including Little Hans' horse (98). What could, to some extent, be understood as an awareness of human epistemological limitations in texts like *Totem and Taboo* and *Civilization and Its Discontents* is, in the very process of psychoanalysing dreams and desires, instead a sign of ignorance about the material, affective roles animals play in human lives (in both psychosexual and social realms). Freudian psychoanalysis may well be following a long history of thought about animals which reduces (or we might say elevates) them to symbolic status, but it displays a distinct eagerness to turn the animals that appear in conscious and unconscious processes into humans. In doing so, a sharp line is drawn between the humans who experience symbolic dreams and the animals that are merely objects of symbolic capture.

Focusing on the phenomena of dreaming, Maud Ellmann raises the additional question of what this means for those humans who don't experience symbolic dimensions to their dreams, like shell-shocked war victims who experience 'literal re-enactments of traumatic events, undisguised by symbolic substitution. If the human is distinguished from the rat by the capacity to dream in tropes, does this mean the traumatized are less than human?' However strange or exceptional this question may on the face of it seem, 'it follows from the premise that human dreams are governed by the logic of symbolic substitution'. At issue here is not, Ellmann adds, 'whether animals can talk, dream, or symbolize, but whether these powers are "proper" or integral to the human'. She concludes that 'since all these powers can be lost, diminished, or disrupted, they cannot be guaranteed as inalienable properties of human minds' (2014: 333). Freudian psychoanalysis may seek to de-centre the human subject, but it is in danger of *re*-centring it elsewhere by using animals as vehicles in the process of arriving at a particular notion of what a healthy or unhealthy human subject is. De-centring human subjectivity doesn't necessarily lead to a non-anthropocentric worldview.

The Imaginary and the Symbolic

Animals fulfil a symbolic role in psychoanalysis on two levels: firstly, they are symbols of human features and concerns; secondly, they are themselves denied this capacity for making meaning out of symbols and therefore represent what the human is not. While Freud's case studies present ample examples of the former, this latter aspect is most evident in the work of Jacques Lacan. Lacan's rich array of essays collected in the *Écrits* occasionally refers to research by ethologists and animal psychologists, but it usually does so to distinguish humans from animals. In his 1946 'Presentation of Psychical Causality', for example, Lacan turns to 'the animal kingdom' in discussing his theory of the types of emotionally charged images humans have of other people – what he terms, in a return to the Latin word, the 'imago' – and how this relates to identification: 'with the imago, psychology had given us a concept which could be at least as fruitful in biology as many other concepts that are far more uncertain but that have nevertheless gained currency there' (2006a: 154). One well-known example he provides is from a 1939 paper by the British zoologist L. Harrison Matthews in *Proceedings of the Royal Society*, which showed that the ovulation of a female pigeon (which doesn't happen when isolated from other members of its species) 'is triggered by a female pigeon's sight of the specific form of a member of its own species, to the exclusion of any other sensory form of perception, and without that member having to be male'. Lacan adds that 'what is more remarkable still is that the mere sight by an animal of its own image in a mirror suffices to trigger ovulation within two and a half months' (154). This suggests that the imago is available to the animal kingdom, but the difference according to Lacan is that this access to the imago doesn't have the profound effect it has for humans – it is simply mimetic. Animals cannot be thought to undergo the same process of subject-formation as humans.

Lacan expands elsewhere on the fundamental difference between humans and animals in terms of their response to mirrors. In 'The Mirror Stage as Formative of the *I* Function', Lacan begins with the fact that 'the human child, at an age when he is for a short while, but for a while nevertheless, outdone by the chimpanzee in instrumental intelligence, can already recognize his own image as such in a mirror' (2006b: 75). The experience of the mirror is markedly different for human infant and chimpanzee: this recognition 'immediately gives rise in a child to a series of gestures in which he playfully experiences the relationship between the movements made in the image and the reflected environment, and between this virtual complex and the reality it duplicates' – this reality being 'the child's own body, and the persons and even things around him' (75). For the chimpanzee, in contrast, this act of recognition exhausts itself. In 'Aggressiveness in Psychoanalysis' Lacan clarifies the distinction:

what demonstrates the phenomenon of recognition, implying subjectivity, are the signs of triumphant jubilation and the playful self-discovery that characterize the child's encounter with his mirror image starting in the sixth month. This behaviour contrasts sharply with the indifference shown by the very animals that perceive this image – the chimpanzee, for example – once they have tested its vanity as an object; and it is even more noteworthy as it occurs at an age when the child lags behind the chimpanzee in instrumental intelligence, only catching up with the latter at eleven months of age. (2006c: 92)

The infant, Lacan emphasises, possesses a kind of intelligence that even the most advanced chimpanzee will never attain because the type of intelligence experienced by chimpanzees is purely 'instrumental' and focused on achieving mechanical tasks rather than being properly the thoughts of a subject. Of course we need to remember that Lacan is using research current at the time – and indeed was more attuned than many of his contemporaries to comparative psychology – even if studies since have shown a richer subjective experience of animals faced with mirrors, or have challenged the view that the mirror test is an appropriate way to measure self-awareness. But the way Lacan frames, measures and interprets is itself revealing. Development is defined here as linear and is judged on human terms (the animal is considered unable to do the things the human can, rather than looking at what the animal *can* do that the human cannot). And animals fail, in Lacan's mind, to experience the mirror as a *stage*, in that it doesn't lead to another phase in the complicated formation of subjectivity and entry into the social realm. The animal may have some (restricted) level of consciousness and self-awareness, but it remains in a *natural* relation to the image. In contrast, the infant experiences a 'transformation' which 'situates the agency known as the ego' before entering the social field – that is, the infant splits from nature in experiencing 'an organic inadequacy of his natural reality' (2006b: 76).

Discussing 'The Mirror Stage' in *The Beast and the Sovereign*, Jacques Derrida reflects on how, when it was first published, Lacan's paper offered hope for a radical displacement of the human/animal binary by taking 'into account a specular function in the sexualization of the animal', something 'quite rare for the time'. And yet it contains one 'massive limitation' in that it oversimplifies animal experience and 'immobilizes the animal forever . . . in the snares of the imaginary'. This entirely deprives animals of 'access to the symbolic', to the unconscious, and so they 'will never be, like man, a "prey to language"' (2009: 113). The animal can never enter the social field, can never move from nature to culture, as does the human, because it is trapped in an imaginary that is untouched by the symbolic order (the laws, rules or norms passed on through language and culture). Lacan's 'The Function and Field of Speech and Language in Psychoanalysis', a paper he delivered in 1953, nicely confirms this point. Lacan pays close attention to the observed phenomenon, studied at great length by the Austrian ethologist Karl von Frisch, whereby:

when a bee returns to its hive after gathering nectar, it transmits an indication of the existence of nectar near or far away from the hive to its companions by two sorts of dances. The second is the most remarkable, for the plan in which the bee traces out a figure-eight – a shape that gave it the name 'wagging dance' – and the frequency of the figures executed within a given time, designate, on the one hand, the exact direction to be followed, determined in relation to the sun's inclination (by which bees are able to orient themselves in all kinds of weather, thanks to their sensitivity to polarized light), and, on the other hand, the distance at which the nectar is to be found up to several miles away. The other bees respond to this message by immediately setting off for the place thus designated. (2006d: 245)

While Lacan agrees that this bee activity 'is certainly a code or signalling system', he questions whether it can be called a language: 'But is it a language, for all that? We can say that it is distinguished from language precisely by the fixed correlation between its signs and the reality they signify' (246). The bee comes to stand for the sign systems of animals in general that more directly relate to the material world than human linguistic signs. Lacan is clearly interested in animal modes of being, but just when he seems poised to radically challenge the Cartesian divide he is instead, as Derrida notes, 'so keen to dissociate the anthropological from the zoological: man is an animal but he speaks' (2009: 113). The real challenge is 'not a matter of "giving speech back"' to animals, but trying to reconceptualise and respond to this seeming lack of speech as not, in fact, a *lack* at all (2008: 48). Doing so might, as discussed more fully in Chapter 3, open up possibilities for other forms of meaning-making and world-making.

In a striking passage in his 1961 seminar on 'Identification', Lacan attempts precisely to give a kind of speech back to his own 'boxer bitch' Justine:

My dog, in a sense and without ambiguity, speaks. My dog has without any doubt the gift of speech. This is important, because it does not mean that she possesses language totally. The measure in which she has speech without having the human relationship to language is a question from which it is worthwhile envisaging the problem of the preverbal. What does my dog do when she speaks, in my sense? Why do I say that she speaks? She does not speak all the time, she speaks contrary to many humans only at moments when she needs to speak. She has a need to speak at moments of emotional intensity and of relationships to the other, to myself, and some other people. This manifests itself by sorts of little guttural whimpers. (1961–2: III 3)

Lacan goes on to outline comparisons between the physiological movements involved in this kind of canine 'speech' and human speech, although his description of this as 'a whole set of mechanisms of a properly phonatory type' has something in common with the Cartesian view of mechanical animal actions. Echoing 'The Mirror Stage', the distinction between human and non-human comes in the 'relationship to identification': 'contrary to what happens in the case of man in so far as he speaks, she [Lacan's boxer] never takes me for another'. That is, whereas humans recognise in others an 'Other with a big O' (through a process called transference), animals always recognise the other with a small 'o' (the other in itself, directly or 'without ambiguity') (III 4–5). Once again, Lacan's discourse plays a 'double role' in that it 'can help us think, but can also fail to help us think or even forbid us to think' about complicated, non-hierarchical relations (Derrida 2009: 102).

Lacan protests that it would be incorrect to view the 'privilege' he grants to language as 'some sort of pride' that masks a 'prejudice which would make of man precisely some sort of summit of being'. Yet too often his descriptions of the incapacity of animals for transference (another way of saying animals lack the symbolic) do betray an assertion of human superiority. Continuing his discussion of Justine, he comments:

> this shapely boxer bitch who, if one is to believe those who observe her has feelings of love for me, gives herself over to fits of passion towards me in which she takes on a quite terrifying aspect for the more timorous souls who exist for example at one or other level of my offspring: it appears that people are afraid that, at the moments that she begins to jump on top of me with her ears flattened and growling in a certain fashion, the fact that she takes my wrists between her teeth might appear to be a threat. This is nevertheless not at all the case. Very quickly, and this is why it is said that she loves me, a few words from me bring her to order, even if I have to repeat myself a few times, and stop the game. (1961–2: III 4)

It is telling that Lacan's own speech here brings the dog 'to order'. It may well be true that pets obey their owners' voices, but the fact that this ordering is Lacan's example of what dog love *is* reinforces the asymmetrical nature of the encounter. To be sure, Lacan's theoretical writings are useful in making sure we don't simply equate animal sign systems with human sign systems; he is aware of some of the different ways animals communicate and doesn't want to reach too readily for anthropomorphic explanations of animal life. But *anthropocentrism* largely prevails as he overlooks the more challenging question of what it would mean for humans to be brought to a kind of order by the *animal's* call.

ANTHROPOMORPHISM: PITFALLS AND POTENTIAL

Psychoanalytic animals often turn out to be all too human. In many instances they are either stand-ins for human concerns, or they are used primarily to confirm, by way of contrast, a specifically human worldview. But can the experiences of animals ever be theorised without being appropriated by human systems of thought? This brings the question of anthropomorphism, and whether it can or should be avoided, to the forefront of animal theory. The challenge is neatly laid out by the feminist theorist Luce Irigaray in her essay 'Animal Compassion':

> How can we talk about them? How can we talk to them? These familiars
> of our existence inhabit another world, a world that I do not know.
> Sometimes I can observe something in it, but I do not inhabit it from
> the inside – it remains foreign to me. The objective signs that appear
> do not bring me the key to the meaning for them, the meaning among
> themselves. Not really, unless I project my human imaginary onto
> them. To make them simple objects of study is not appropriate any
> more than to make them partners of a universe that they do not share.
> (2004: 195)

Here Irigaray repeatedly emphasises a gulf between humans and the animals who inhabit 'another world' that can only be penetrated through a projection of the 'human imaginary'. The imaginative act of trying to explain their world runs the risk of becoming a kind of lie. We could say there is a respect from Irigaray towards animal worlds in that she shows an awareness that animals have a world of their own. But the question remains as to how true it is to conclude that we can never penetrate animals' experiences.

What is it Like to be an Animal?

This question is addressed in the American philosopher Thomas Nagel's well-known 1974 article 'What is it Like to be a Bat?' Arguing against reductive materialist accounts of the mind that ignore the complexity of subjective experience, Nagel outlines that consciousness is a 'widespread phenomenon' that 'occurs at many levels of animal life'. It is his belief in a widespread array of conscious experience that leads Nagel to ask the specific question that forms the title of his essay: 'no matter how the form may vary, the fact that an organism has conscious experience *at all* means, basically, that there is something it is like to be that organism'. He adds that 'fundamentally an organism has conscious mental states if and only if there is something that it is to *be* that organism' (1979: 166). An issue we might immediately raise is whether the 'something' that 'it is like' to be an 'organism' is more or less accessible to human minds depending on what that organism is. In other words, if we are going to imagine the world of a particular animal, does it make a difference which one? Are we more likely to know the conscious experience of a monkey than a goldfish? A dolphin than a mouse? Nagel suggests that 'if one travels too far down the phylogenetic tree' people will be less likely to believe there is any experience in the animal at all, and so he settles on bats as an example of highly evolved mammals that 'nevertheless present a range of activity and a sensory apparatus' that is thoroughly distinct – indeed 'fundamentally *alien*' – from humans (168).

Nagel argues that the subjective experiences of humans are not conducive to finding a method through which the subjective experiences of other animals can be accessed:

> Our own experience provides the basic material for our imagination, whose range is therefore limited. It will not help to try to imagine that one has webbing on one's arms, which enables one to fly around at dusk and dawn catching insects in one's mouth; that one has very poor vision, and perceives the surrounding world by a system of reflected high-frequency sound signals; and that one spends the day hanging upside down by one's feet in an attic. In so far as I can imagine this (which is not very far), it tells me only what it would be like for me to behave as a bat behaves. But that is not the question. I want to know what it is like for a *bat* to be a bat. Yet if I try to imagine this, I am restricted to the resources of my own mind, and those resources are inadequate to the task. I cannot perform it either by imagining additions to my present experience, or by imagining segments gradually subtracted from it, or by imagining some combination of additions, subtractions, and modifications. (169)

It is not enough to imaginatively mimic a bat (or any other animal) in order to understand their experience of the world. This would create a falsely animalised human perspective which, because still rooted in human experience, will in turn reveal a humanised view of animal life. In imagining animal experience the human cannot help but judge the animal based on human qualities. Although Nagel doesn't use the term in his paper, we can understand his discussion to be one that worries about the pitfalls of anthropomorphism.

What is emphasised here is that if we have a subjective conceptual system and a distinctly human language, then we cannot possibly know what it is like to be a bat or, for that matter, any other animal. Yet Nagel doesn't deal in absolutes in his paper. It is not simply a case of saying we can never know *anything* of animal experience because the specific animal in question might vary – animals are not a homogeneous pack. Nagel conceives of this kind of knowledge of the animal's experience as a sliding scale where the 'distance between oneself and other persons and other species can fall anywhere on a continuum'. Humans have their place on this scale, where we cannot, strictly speaking, know what it is like to be another human (even though we may know what it is like for us to *act like* another human). Destined to deal in 'partial' knowledge, humans don't have an infinite capacity for understanding (172). When we take into account the multiplicity of differences between species as well as within species, the difficulty of the task is furthered. To remain with the example of bats, 'if you lined up each kind of mammal living on earth today,' writes ethologist Jonathan Balcombe, 'every fourth one would be a bat. There are more than a thousand species, which ranks them second only to rodents in diversity among the twenty-nine living mammal groups' (2010: 9). The question of what it is like to be a bat is further complicated and seemingly impossible to grasp because bats themselves are such a diverse species.

Nagel can be read as presenting an awareness of the limitations of human imagination. The worry about the coupling of anthropocentrism and anthropo-morphism means he is sceptical, like Freud in *Civilization and Its Discontents*, about the human's ability to know what it is like to be an animal. And there is no doubt that Nagel's scepticism guards against both dismissive anthro-pocentrism and extravagant anthropomorphism (the latter of which would, in the end, perhaps tell us more about human imaginative projections than about actual animals). But there are problems with this approach that relate to Nagel's very framing of the issue. Contained within the question 'What is it like to be a bat?', the words 'like' and 'be' present a tension between the figurative and literal, imagination and reality. Moreover, as Mark Payne writes in *The Animal Part*, 'Nagel's assertion of impossibility rests on a contrast between successful and unsuccessful imagining.' We can reverse Nagel's ques-tion and ask what it would mean 'to imagine being a bat . . . unsuccessfully? For Nagel it means to not have the perceptual experience of a bat, but this is to not be a bat, not to fail to imagine being one' (Payne 2010: 14). For Payne, on the contrary, the role of 'empathetic imagination' can actually open up less anthropocentric ways to think about and treat creatures such as bats. If we are to suspect the human imagination because it doesn't allow us to replicate the sensory systems of other animals and therefore experience exactly what they do, then we miss out on numerous imaginative possibilities that might reveal insight into the experiences of animals and challenge false assumptions about both humans and nonhumans. What is gained through the suspicion of human attempts to imagine the lives of others is more than matched by what is lost. A central and perhaps more profound question arises: is there a way to think about the figurative and literal, imagination and reality not in opposition to one another, but in alliance? Put differently, is there a way to disentangle anthropomorphism from anthropocentrism?

Alternative Anthropomorphisms

Many animal theorists now argue that it is important to remain open to the potential in anthropomorphism, and that closing down discussions, even when they are based on efforts to point out the limitations of human knowledge, leads to a sometimes inadvertent, sometimes wilful, ignorance of animality. Instead of always already aligning anthropomorphism with anthropocentrism, a rich debate has emerged, exemplified by the essays in *Thinking with Animals: New Perspectives on Anthropomorphism*, edited by Lorraine Daston and Gregg Mitman, about the potential for anthropomorphism to challenge human superiority and the rigid distinctions that are made between human and animal experience. In her insightful essay in the volume, Daston concedes that 'humans face great, perhaps insurmountable obstacles when they try to understand what it would be like to be a nonhuman', but she is nevertheless interested in the ways that sustained efforts have been made to 'escape anthropomorphism' and 'think one's way into truly other minds' (2005: 38). Focusing on very distinct traditions that have markedly different aims – namely medieval angelology and comparative psychology from the late nineteenth and early twentieth century – Daston delineates parallels that allow us to see how complex the issue of anthropomorphism is when placed in historical context:

> Both traditions regarded anthropomorphism as a formidable threat to their undertakings . . . To apply human categories to God, and even to the separated intelligences commonly known as angels, was recognized by medieval theologians to be at once risky and inevitable – much the same predicament articulated by the post-Darwinian comparative psychologists. Both psychologists and theologians relied on analogy to bridge the unbridgeable . . . both theologians and psychologists were centrally interested in two aspects of the human/nonhuman comparison: thought and feeling. Do angels feel sadness? Can they recognize individuals? Do animals have concepts? Are they bitten by remorse? In both cases, inquiries into the mental world of nonhumans served to sharpen and refine notions of human understanding and emotion. (39)

Daston's approach serves as an important reminder that what we mean by anthropomorphism, as well as our conceptualisation of mental life, has vastly changed over time. For the comparative psychologists, everything is divided into the 'subjective' and 'objective'. Because twentieth-century thought was

[handwritten marginal notes:] Since death itself is entire/so other to life, it would seem impossible for life itself to understand, glimpse, prepare for, or even death. But the other in the animal is just as other as death this is why the one of many more realistic entry point into thinking about death.

so influenced by this approach, in order to answer questions posed by analytic philosophers like Nagel it is thought that one has to construct the conscious experiences of nonhuman animals. Nagel's discussion is based on the assumptions that knowing what it is like to be an animal is about understanding 'conscious mental states' and 'the subjective character of experience' (1979: 40). In contrast, medieval theologians of angelology did not base their thought on the same subject/object split and the 'anthropos' (human) and 'morphos' (form) were entirely different concepts in the middle ages than they were in the twentieth century (Daston 2005: 40).

Nagel's question of what it is like to be a bat is therefore based on conceptualisations of subjective consciousness, perspective and sympathy that are historically specific. When we link anthropomorphism to anthropocentrism, we are doing so because we still think from within the confines of 'a world divided up into the objective and the subjective' (Daston 2005: 53). When we foreground 'the method of sympathetic projection' this leads us to think that 'understanding another mind could only mean seeing with another's eyes (or smelling with another's nose or hearing with another's sonar, depending on the species)'. That the question should become one of individual experience is based on numerous cultural and intellectual shifts – in religion, literature, psychology, politics, economics – that have inflated the importance of individuality. As Daston notes: 'No medieval theologian would ever have recommended adopting the perspective of an angel in order to understand the angelic mind, any more than a specialist in artificial intelligence would attempt to adopt the computer's point of view' (53). The emphasis placed by thinkers like Nagel on subjective experience comes from a sense that all subjects experience the external objective world from different individual *perspectives*. The subject/object distinction has become so crucial in modern thought that 'it is hard to conceive of alternative ways of posing the question of how to understand nonhuman minds except in terms of objective behaviour and subjective consciousness'. In an attempt to re-frame the discussion, Daston therefore asks: 'If understanding other minds, both human and nonhuman, were not about probing alien subjectivities, that is, vicariously experiencing strange states of consciousness, what would it be about?' (40) It is only via a consideration of this question – which involves exploring multiple modes of being and probing what it is to have experience in the world at all, topics investigated at length in Chapters 2 and 3 – that animal theorists might gain greater knowledge of animality.

There are many signs that contemporary approaches to animal life across disciplines are open to the possibility of an anthropomorphism that is disentangled from anthropocentrism, and the insight that might be gained from this. In *The Emotional Lives of Animals*, ecologist and ethologist Marc Bekoff goes as far as stating that anthropomorphism is a 'necessity' if we are to try to understand animal consciousness, but cautions that it 'must be done carefully, consciously, empathetically, and biocentrically'. To anthropomorphise biocentrically is to 'make every attempt to maintain the animal's point of view' (Bekoff 2007: 125). In contemporary philosophy, Jane Bennett affirms the potential of a biocentric anthropomorphism as part of her attempt in *Vibrant Matter* to discuss the lively materiality of nonhuman experience:

> an anthropomorphic element in perception can uncover a whole world of resonances and resemblances – sounds and sights that echo and bounce far more than would be possible were the universe to have a hierarchical structure . . . A touch of anthropomorphism, then, can catalyze a sensibility that finds a world filled not with ontologically distinct categories of beings (subjects and objects) but with variously composed materialities that form confederations. In revealing similarities across categorical divides and lighting up structural parallels between material forms in 'nature' and those in 'culture,' anthropomorphism can reveal isomorphisms. (2010: 99)

Carefully approached, anthropomorphism can provide a useful mode of conceptualising multiple agencies that are not human, and in the process can 'counter the narcissism of humans in charge of the world' (xvi).

Viewed in this way anthropomorphism is not only set against anthropocentrism, but also begins to call into question the very term itself. For in naming the process of articulating experiences of animals as 'anthropomorphism' we implicitly assume that the functions and features we are discussing belong solely to humans. As Erica Fudge argues, anthropomorphism 'might actually be unfairly naming something that is not so human-centric. Maybe animals are more like us than we want to imagine and the label "anthropomorphism" merely allows us to recognize this and devalue it simultaneously.' Our use of the very word 'anthropomorphism' can in fact work to 'undercut the dangerous possibility that the gap between human and animal is not so large after all' (2002: 144). What is needed is a conceptualisation of anthropomorphism that is aware of the possibility of its own *non*-anthropomorphism.

WRITING 'AS IF' ANTHROPOMORPHISM: 'LIZZIE'S TIGER'

Literary fiction provides an ideal form to consider the pitfalls and potential of anthropomorphism. Reading animals in fiction demands interpretative strategies that are attentive to different uses of language and the multiple meanings that can be attached to words. There is certainly a way to read animals in literature as stand-ins for human thoughts and feelings much as Freud does when interpreting dreams and phobias. This has been the dominant way of thinking about literary animals – they are symbolic, metaphorical or allegorical instruments used for explorations of the human psyche or commentaries on themes like gender, race and class. While such readings of animals can provide insight into how they enter the human's symbolic order, they are also examples of where an animal becomes something other than an animal. One mode of thought, following Nagel, would be that the life of an animal cannot be captured and therefore any imaginative exploration of animals in literature would be fantastical, something to be confined to 'fiction' in the strictest sense of the word. But if there is a another way to consider the relationship between humans and animals that gives a kind of voice to the animal, how might this be expressed?

Angela Carter's 1981 short story 'Lizzie's Tiger' offers a fascinating example of the complicated negotiation offered by writers who attempt to articulate the shared experiences of human and nonhuman animals. It is written as the prequel to Carter's earlier story, 'The Fall River Axe Murders', which is based on the true life story of American Lizzie Borden (1860–1927) who was notoriously charged, tried and then acquitted of the 1892 axe-murders of her father and stepmother in Fall River, Massachusetts. To this day the case remains unsolved, although Carter's story indicates that Lizzie committed the murders. One striking aspect of this earlier story is the way in which the narrator links, as a potential reason for the murder, violence towards animals and patriarchal rule, a theme investigated in more detail in Chapter 4. Lizzie was an animal lover, and we are told 'she would like a pet, a kitten or a puppy, she loves small animals and birds, too' and that she kept pigeons in the loft and would 'feed them grain out of the palms of her cupped hands' (1996a: 376; 378). Yet her father kills her pigeons and her stepmother wants to eat them: 'Old Borden took a dislike to their cooing, it got on his nerves . . . one afternoon he took out the hatchet from the woodpile in the cellar and chopped those pigeons' heads right off, he did' (378). Her stepmother 'fancied the slaughtered pigeons for a pie'. On discovering this 'Lizzie went down to inspect the instrument of destruction. She picked it up and weighed it in her hand' (378). We never read of Lizzie using the hatchet, but the implication is that the tyrannical combination of patriarchal rule and this violence against the pigeons was too much for her to take. Lizzie appears to feel an alliance with these animals.

In 'Lizzie's Tiger', animals are more prominent still. Carter returns to the four-year-old Lizzie in a move that might initially seem to be about seeking explanations for her adult actions in her childhood development. One way to read the encounter would be as a kind of case study akin to the work of Freud or Klein. At the beginning of the story the young child sneaks out one night from a house (that was more like 'a slum') and eventually makes her way to a circus that is in town. There, animality and sexuality are contained in close proximity, evident when Lizzie is assaulted by a man who 'took firm hold of her right hand and brought it tenderly up between his squatting thighs' (1996b: 383; 389). What Lizzie really takes issue with is the man's desire to be kissed by her – 'He hissed between his teeth: "Kissy, kissy from Missy?"' – which she associates with her father and sister: 'She did mind that and shook an obdurate head; she did not like her father's hard, dry, imperative kisses, and endured them only for the sake of power. Sometimes Emma touched her cheek lightly with unparted lips. Lizzie would allow no more' (389). When the feline protagonist appears, from a psychoanalytic perspective this tiger would act as a human substitute: either for the mother, where it could be seen as part of a 'blissful pre-oedipal encounter, echoing the union between mother and child beyond the reach of the father and the paternal law' (Müller-Wood 2004: 290); or alternatively for the father (the tiger's tail is, after all, 'thick as her father's forearm' [391]). The tiger may even point to the daughter's desires for her father in a kind of neo-Freudian 'Electra complex', the girl's version of the Oedipus complex. But as Janet Langlois notes, this 'phallic (and paternal) connection' is too 'obvious and overblown' to be taken seriously and has more to do with Carter 'parodying Freudians' projective readings' (1998: 204). The tiger and the other animals in Carter's story are linked to her relations with her family, with whom she lives in an almost claustrophobic atmosphere, but these animals become involved in the story in important ways *as animals* and don't simply act as symbolic humans. Indeed, the animals in this story are partly about an escape from a formation of knowledge that relies on neat psychoanalytic paradigms that won't allow for the intensive encounter between human and animal. Instead of remaining confined to a human Oedipal drama, Carter is interested in material encounters between Lizzie and the animals in the story, as well as in exploring the divide between species.

Before arriving at the circus – itself an arena of anthropocentrism – Lizzie is accompanied by domestic animals that are under human rule: in her home, where she has lived with her father and older sister since her mother died, she is surrounded by 'howling dogs who, since puppyhood, had known of the world only the circumference of their chain' (1996b: 384). On sneaking outside a small cat appears to want to halt Lizzie's own escape from her domestic sphere: 'The cat put out a paw as Lizzie brushed past, as if seeking to detain her, as if to suggest she took second thoughts as to her escapade' (385). This passage is especially significant because it introduces the connective 'as if' that is frequently used by Carter in her representation of animals. The sentence is clearly anthropomorphic, where human motives and thoughts are projected onto the cat. But the 'as if' draws attention to this anthropomorphism as an imaginative possibility rather than a certain judgement. The uncertainty and conditionality in 'as if' presents an added hesitation in the attempt to find a rhythm that expresses the relationship between human and nonhuman, offering one way in which figurative language need not signal appropriation of the animal but might allow for a subtle, careful speculation about nonhuman experience.

While this 'as if' allows for a tentative exploration of the life of those domestic animals we are familiar with through everyday experiences (a relationship discussed in detail in Chapter 3), it becomes more significant when Lizzie reaches the circus and encounters more exotic animals. On first coming face-to-face with the tiger who, we are left in no doubt, has been imprisoned ('Upon its pelt it bore the imprint of the bars behind which it lived'), Lizzie experiences a sense of the unknowable: 'The tiger kept its head down; questing hither and thither though in quest of what might not be told' (391). We read that this tiger moves in a 'mysterious patrol' (392). Faced with unknowability, the two most obvious choices confronting the narrator at this point are: to accept the unknowability of the animal and therefore not bother with speculation and instead focus on the human character's response; or, to simply treat the animal character like any human character and ascribe its thoughts and actions in the same manner. These approaches to writing animals would be in danger of either ignoring the animality of the animal altogether, or running the risk of matching the material capture of the animal with a symbolic one, whereby anthropomorphism transforms the animal into a human. Drawing attention to this difficulty of writing the animal, both of these options are presented to Carter's readers in the story, where what seems to be anthropomorphic projections about the tiger's mental state in one paragraph is followed in the next by an assertion that in fact the tiger was unknowable:

> Then something strange happened. The svelte beast fell to its knees.
> It was as if it had been subdued by the presence of this child, as if this
> little child of all the children in the world, might lead it towards a
> peaceable kingdom where it need not eat meat. But only 'as if'. All we
> could see was, it knelt. A crackle of shock ran through the tent; the tiger
> was acting out of character.
>
>   Its mind remained, however, a law unto itself. We did not know what
> it was thinking. How could we? (392)

From the first sentence when 'something strange happened', we are aware that we are entering an encounter that will somehow be other than expected. The very act of writing about this encounter is stranger still in that it involves writing about an animal that is itself a stranger to language. This is where Carter's use of figurative language, and in particular the connective 'as if', is crucial. By repeating 'as if' in this passage, Carter's narrator actually marks a mode of story-telling that moves tentatively between anthropomorphism and anthropocentrism. Writing 'as if' anthropomorphism is to present a *non-anthropocentric* anthropomorphism.

This more careful, speculative but serious anthropomorphism is articulated in the following paragraphs: 'it came towards her, as if she were winding it to her on an invisible string by the exercise of pure will' (392). The 'as if' here begins to doubt not only the tiger's motivations but the very idea of the 'pure will' of Lizzie – it almost mocks the notion that the human can hold such a strong force. The following admission by the narrator is apt: 'I cannot tell you how much she loved this tiger, nor how wonderful she thought it was.' We have moved here from the unknowability of the animal to the unknowability of the human child. Knowledge, it is implied, exceeds language, for how can words really capture what a child is thinking? Can thoughts be reducible to language? We have moved from a human perspective on the animal other, to an 'othering' of both that acknowledges they are equally strangers to the reader and to each other; 'they never took their eyes off one another, though neither had the least idea what the other meant' (392). If there is any anthropomorphism here, it is employed to uproot our preconceived ideas of what is human and what is animal; identity becomes something that emerges *from* this encounter rather than being fixed to subjects *before* they enter it.

This also recalls a passage from 'The Fall River Axe Murders', when the narrator uses the 'as if' connective to explain why Lizzie rejected an invitation to be away from Fall River on the day of the murder: 'Lizzie was invited away, too, to a summer house by the sea to join a merry band of girls but, as if on purpose to mortify her flesh, as if important business kept her in the exhausted town, as if a wicked fairy spelled her in Second Street, she did not go' (1996a: 361). The repetition of 'as if' here is twice removed from 'fact': it signals a figurative, imaginative realm as well as being uncertain about this imagination. These three reasons are, as Anja Müller-Wood argues, 'fantasies imagined by the many Fall River amateur detectives trying to come to grips with that puzzle located in their midst' but are also 'metafictional signals reminding all too trusting readers that this text is an assemblage of subjective and hence unreliable positions' (2004: 284). Both of Carter's stories make a wider point about not just the (un)knowability of animals but the (un)knowability of humans.

The flawed assumption that human knowledge transcends animality is exposed in 'Lizzie's Tiger' when the encounter between Lizzie and the tiger is interrupted by a man who claims superior knowledge: 'The spell broke', and with that this speculative exploration of crossing the divide between human and nonhuman is destroyed:

A lash cracked round the tiger's carnivorous head, and a glorious hero sprang into the age brandishing in the hand that did not hold the whip

a three-legged stool. He wore fawn breeches, black boots, a bright
red jacket frogged with gold, a tall hat. A dervish, he; he beckoned,
crouched, pointed with the whip, menaced with the stool, leaped and
twirled in a brilliant ballet of mimic ferocity, the dance of the Taming
of the Tiger, to whom the tamer gave no chance to fight at all. (1996b:
392–3)

The darkly ironic description of the tamer as a 'glorious hero' who 'twirled in
a brilliant ballet' portrays a scene of human violence against an animal, which
allows no room for the kind of interaction shared by Lizzie and the tiger earlier
in the story. The following paragraphs stage a straightforward anthropomorphism, which contrasts sharply with the subtlety and boundary-blurring of
the previous encounter. We read of the tiger's 'confusion' and 'humiliation'
at being violently whipped by the ironically titled tamer (393). The use of 'as
if', and along with it the attempt to open up imaginative possibilities towards
the animal or to form a connection across species, is replaced by a material
and symbolic violence. As the tamer then 'cleared his throat for speech' – the
capacity that is so often seen to hierarchically separate human from animal –
we are told: 'He was a hero. He was a tiger himself, but even more so, because
he was a man.' We shouldn't be mistaken in thinking the man has in any way
become animal here; the tiger was denied its animality by this man from the
beginning by being reduced to 'docility and obedience'. Instead, the animal
has been subsumed by the man: the 'tiger' in him is an anthropocentric and
anthropomorphic concept that he has captured 'because he was a man'. Even
when an emotion is drawn on that is supposedly shared by the man and the
tiger, there is little interest in the understanding of the animal. For the tamer
the bond between man and beast is simply an anthropomorphic fear that is
about his own existential angst: 'I'm not half so scared of the big brute as it is
of me!' The focus on fear – an emotion notably absent from Lizzie's encounter
– by the tamer represents the violence of man's so-called 'rational' attitude: 'I
bring to bear upon its killer instinct a rational man's knowledge of the power
of fear . . . I have established a hierarchy of FEAR' (394).

The circus is the arena of 'man'. When we learn that the tamer is the very
man who had earlier thrust his drunken sexuality so disturbingly upon Lizzie,
a man who 'exhibited such erect mastery', it is clear that anthropocentrism
and phallocentrism are both on display (394). Lizzie's encounter with the tiger
is quite different. While the story's title, 'Lizzie's Tiger', may suggest human
possession of the animal, it becomes clear that the story is, in Mary Pollock's
words, about an 'emotional alliance'. This alliance is not 'based on the sentimental or totemic identification with animals . . . Instead the actions of both
the child and the tiger are intentional, valid, "common sense" responses to
the connecting systems of dominance and control in which they are trapped'

(2000: 47). This story shows us that Lizzie's shared sympathy with animals is set against the tyranny of patriarchal rule. As such, it puts into sharp focus the scene in 'The Fall River Axe Murders' when Lizzie's father kills the pigeons, those other animals she had bonded with. When the violent performance is over in 'Lizzie's Tiger', everyone returns home seemingly unmoved: the audience 'soon got bored with watching the tiger splintering the wooden stool, and drifted off' (1996b: 395). Everyone except Lizzie, that is. After this transformative, traumatic encounter, she must return to her patriarchal familial arena: 'her cover broke . . . half the remaining gawpers in the tent had kin been bleakly buried by her father, the rest owed him money. She was the most famous daughter in all Fall River.' The story is transformed for the reader when at this moment we learn for the first time that this is the same Lizzie Borden from Carter's earlier 'Fall River' story. Now 'out of her disguise of dirt and silence' (396) she is captured in her own circus of civilisation.

KEY TEXTS

Carter, Angela (1996a), 'The Fall River Axe Murders', in *Burning Your Boats: Collected Stories*, London: Vintage, pp. 359–79.

Carter, Angela (1996b), 'Lizzie's Tiger', in *Burning Your Boats: Collected Stories*, London: Vintage, pp. 383–96.

Daston, Lorraine (2005), 'Intelligences: Angelic, Animal, Human', in Lorraine Daston and Gregg Mitman (eds), *Thinking with Animals: New Perspectives Anthropomorphism*, New York: Columbia University Press, pp. 37–58.

Daston, Lorraine and Gregg Mitman (eds) (2005), *Thinking with Animals: New Perspectives on Anthropomorphism*, New York: Columbia University Press.

Freud, Sigmund (1960), *Totem and Taboo: Some Points of Agreement Between the Mental Lives of Savages and Neurotics*, trans. James Strachey, London: Routledge.

Freud, Sigmund (1977), *Case Histories 1: 'Dora' and 'Little Hans'*, Pelican Freud Library vol. 8, Harmondsworth: Pelican.

Freud, Sigmund (1997), *The Interpretation of Dreams*, trans. A. A. Brill, Hertfordshire: Wordsworth.

Freud, Sigmund (2001), 'A Difficulty in Psycho-Analysis', in James Strachey (ed.), *The Standard Edition of the Complete Psychological Works of Sigmund Freud*, vol. 17, London: Vintage, pp. 135–44.

Freud, Sigmund (2004), *Civilization and Its Discontents*, trans. David McLintock, London: Penguin.

Lacan, Jacques (2006a), 'Presentation of Psychical Causality', in *Écrits*, trans. Bruce Fink, New York: W. W. Norton & Company, pp. 123–60.

Lacan, Jacques (2006b), 'The Mirror Stage as Formative of the *I* Function', in *Écrits*, trans. Bruce Fink, New York: W. W. Norton & Company, pp. 75–81.

Lacan, Jacques (2006c), 'Aggressiveness in Psychoanalysis', in *Écrits*, trans. Bruce Fink, New York: W. W. Norton & Company, pp. 82–101.

Lacan, Jacques (2006d), 'The Function and Field of Speech and Language in Psychoanalysis', in *Écrits*, trans. Bruce Fink, New York: W. W. Norton & Company, pp. 197–268.

Nagel, Thomas (1979), 'What is it Like to be a Bat?', in *Mortal Questions*, Cambridge: Cambridge University Press, pp. 265–80.

FURTHER READING

Balcombe, Jonathan (2010), *Second Nature: The Inner Lives of Animals*, New York: Palgrave Macmillan.

Bekoff, Marc (2007), *The Emotional Lives of Animals*, California: New World Library.

Bennett, Jane (2010), *Vibrant Matter: A Political Ecology of Things*, Durham NC: Duke University Press.

Darwin, Charles (2009a), *On the Origin of Species*, London: Penguin.

Darwin, Charles (2009b), *The Expression of the Emotions in Man and Animals*, London: Penguin.

Deleuze, Gilles and Félix Guattari (2004), *Anti-Oedipus: Capitalism and Schizophrenia*, trans. Robert Hurley, Mark Seem and Helen R. Lane, London: Continuum.

Deleuze, Gilles, Félix Guattari, Claire Parnet and André Scala (2007), 'The Interpretation of Utterances', in Gilles Deleuze, *Two Regimes of Madness: Texts and Interviews 1975–1995*, trans. Ames Hodges and Mike Taormina, New York: Semiotext(e), pp. 89–112.

Derrida, Jacques (2008), *The Animal That Therefore I Am*, trans. David Wills, New York: Fordham University Press.

Derrida, Jacques (2009), *The Beast and the Sovereign*, vol. 1, trans. Geoffrey Bennington, Chicago: University of Chicago Press.

Derrida, Jacques (2011), *The Beast and the Sovereign*, vol. 2, trans. Geoffrey Bennington, Chicago: University of Chicago Press.

Ellmann, Maud (2014), 'Psychoanalytic Animal', in Laura Marcus and Ankhi Mukherjee (eds), *A Concise Companion to Psychoanalysis, Literature, and Culture*, Chichester: John Wiley & Sons, pp. 328–50.

Fudge, Erica (2002), *Animal*, London: Reaktion.

Genosko, Gary (1993), 'Freud's Bestiary: How Does Psychoanalysis Treat Animals?', *Psychoanalytic Review* 80.4, 603–32.

Irigaray, Luce (2004), 'Animal Compassion', in Peter Atterton and Matthew

Calarco (eds), *Animal Philosophy: Ethics and Identity*, London: Continuum, pp. 195–201.

Klein, Melanie (1984), *Narrative of a Child Analysis: The Conduct of the Psycho-Analysis of Children as Seen in the Treatment of a Ten-year-old Boy*, London: The Hogarth Press.

Lacan, Jacques (1961–2), *The Seminar of Jacques Lacan*, Book IX Identification, trans. Cormac Gallagher; at <http://www.valas.fr/IMG/pdf/THE-SEMINAR-OF-JACQUES-LACAN-IX_identification.pdf> (accessed 15 December 2014).

Langlois, Janet L. (1998), 'Andrew Borden's Little Girl: Fairy-Tale Fragments in Angela Carter's "The Fall River Axe Murders" and "Lizzie's Tiger"', *Marvels and Tales: Journal of Fairy Tale Studies* 12.1, 192–212.

Müller-Wood, Anja (2004), 'Disconcerting Mirrors: Angela Carter's Lizzie Borden Stories', *LIT: Literature Interpretation Theory* 15.3, 277–97.

Oliver, Kelly (2009a), 'Answering the Call of Nature: Lacan Walking the Dog', in *Animal Lessons: How They Teach Us to Be Human*, New York: Columbia University Press, pp. 175–92.

Oliver, Kelly (2009b), 'Psychoanalysis as Animal By-product: Freud's Zoophilia', in *Animal Lessons: How They Teach Us to Be Human*, New York: Columbia University Press, pp. 247–76.

Payne, Mark (2010), *The Animal Part: Human and Other Animals in the Poetic Imagination*, Chicago: University of Chicago Press.

Pollock, Mary S. (2000), 'Angela Carter's Animal Tales: Constructing the Non-Human', *LIT: Literature Interpretation Theory* 11.1, 35–57.

Ray, Nicholas (2012), 'Psychoanalysis and "The Animal": A Reading of the Metapsychology of Jean Laplanche', *Journal for Critical Animal Studies* 10.1, 40–66.

Ray, Nicholas (2014), 'Interrogating the Human/Animal Relation in Freud's *Civilization and its Discontents*', *Humanimalia* 6.1, 10–40.

Schwab, Gabriele (ed.) (2007), *Derrida, Deleuze, Psychoanalysis*, New York: Columbia University Press.

Seshadri-Crooks, Kaplana (2003), 'Being Human: Bestiality, Anthropophagy, and Law', *Umbr(a): A Journal of the Unconscious* 1, 97–114.

Suen, Alison (2013), 'From Animal Father to Animal Mother: A Freudian Account of Animal Maternal Ethics', *philoSOPHIA: A Journal of Continental Feminism*, 3.2, 121–37.

CHAPTER 2

Animal Ontology

HUMANS AS ANIMALS

When thinking about humans *as* animals, the relationship between human being and animal being is most commonly characterised by both a hierarchical and a supplementary arrangement. That is, the human is seen as the *highest* kind of animal and it is viewed in this way because of what the human *adds* to its base animal being. The eighteenth-century German philosopher Immanuel Kant provides us with one of the clearest examples of this model of the animality of the human, when in his 1797 book *The Metaphysics of Morals* he describes humanity rising above 'mere animality' because the human is 'an animal endowed with reason' (1996: 160; 204). Humanity adds the capacity of reason to animality, and as such it has the ability for end-oriented action: 'The capacity to set oneself an end – any end whatsoever – is what characterizes humanity (as distinguished from animality).' Being human depends upon the ability to enter culture instead of being confined to nature; to 'cultivate the crude predispositions of his nature, by which the animal is first raised into the human being' (154). It follows that animality is the lower part of humanity, and that the human becomes truly human by rising above its animality. In addition, Kant states that any moral concern we have for animals is indirect, and is primarily a concern with not weakening 'morality in one's relations with other men' (192–3).

Set against this viewpoint, where animality is reduced to the base level of humanity and therefore to the background of philosophical thought, another German philosopher, Friedrich Nietzsche, offers a radical break from this hierarchical and supplementary model of the human animal. Writing in the following century, Nietzsche provides a sustained and rigorous attempt to articulate the animality of humans as a virtue. As will become clear, Nietzsche's philosophy is not without its anthropomorphic moments, when the animal is attributed human thoughts and features. But on so many occasions animality is at the foreground rather than background of his thoughts about what it means to be human. Rather than judging animality to be something that must be overcome in order to enter a distinctly human realm, Nietzsche sees *humanity* as that from which we need to be freed. In contrast again to Kant, Nietzsche doesn't hold humans up as moral beings above the animals that have no claim to direct moral consideration. This is confirmed in the following aphorism from his 1881 book *Daybreak*: "'Humanity'. – We do not regard the animals as moral beings. But do you suppose the animals regard us as moral beings? – An animal which could speak said: "Humanity is a prejudice of which we animals at least are free"' (1982: 162). For Nietzsche a 'prejudice' is anything that inflates the human's sense of importance and superiority, and so in *The Gay Science*, published the following year, we find the third of the 'Four Errors' that 'man' has been built on is that 'he felt himself in a false position in relation to the animals and nature' (2006: 86). Nietzsche's philosophical project seeks to undercut reverence for the very concept of humanity.

Instead of viewing human culture as distinct from an animal nature (which would maintain the oppositional relation between an always animal nature and an always human culture), Nietzsche argues for a conceptualisation of culture that is open to, and grounded upon, nature. As he puts it in his early essay 'Homer's Contest':

> If we speak of *humanity*, it is on the basic assumption that it should be that which *separates* man from nature and is his mark of distinction. But in reality there is no such separation: 'natural' characteristics and those called specifically 'human' have grown together inextricably. Man, at the finest height of his powers, is all nature and carries nature's uncanny dual character in himself. His dreadful capabilities and those counting as inhuman are perhaps, indeed, the fertile soil from which alone all humanity, in feelings, deeds and works, can grow forth. (2007: 174)

Human nature is, then, marked as much by an 'inhuman' nature as by an elevated culture. What Nietzsche proposes is less a return to a naive state of nature, in which our actions and identities are merely the result of biologistic properties, and more an understanding of culture that is 'inextricably' connected to embodied existence. Far from considering the animality of the human to be that which never reaches culture, Nietzsche's concern is with 'a cultivation of animality', where culture is defined not by 'moral and rational improvement of the human being' but by critiquing the 'techniques of domination' promoted in the name of civilisation (Lemm 2009: 4; 11). As Vanessa Lemm argues in her astute reading of Nietzsche, 'the task of culture is to free the human animal from the prejudices of civilization' (13). Where Kant implies that cultivation is the process that overcomes the inhumanity of nature and allows the human to reach an improved civilisation, Nietzsche views cultivation as that which overcomes the limits or constrictions of civilisation. According to Nietzsche, 'the animal must emerge again' (1998: 26).

Cultivating Animal Territories

In *The Beast and the Sovereign*, Jacques Derrida refers to Nietzsche's best-known work *Thus Spoke Zarathustra* as 'one of the richest bestiaries in the Western philosophical library' (2009: 3). But on first encountering this bestiary it can appear that Nietzsche's animal figures are mere substitutes for human emotions and attributes. Examples are plentiful from the beginning of the book. In 'Of the Three Metamorphoses' the camel is the 'beast of burden' who stands for the 'weight-bearing spirit' and the lion stands for courage and 'freedom for new creation' (Nietzsche 2003a: 54–5). In 'Of the Chairs of Virtue' Zarathustra is 'patient as a cow', an apparently straightforward simile (57). In 'Of Immaculate Perception' the snake's biblical association with squalor, cunning and danger is apparent, albeit the description is blasphemously used to describe contemplators of god as 'serpent-filth' with 'evil odour' and 'a lizard's cunning' (146) – more often the snake is the 'wisest animal' in an equally blasphemous inversion of Genesis (53, 279). And, in 'Of Old and New Law-Tables' the 'creeping and subtle' worm is associated with those men who are 'parasites' (225). Most troubling is the role of the ape: it is a 'laughing-stock or a painful embarrassment' (41–2); 'superfluous people' who desire wealth and power are described as 'nimble apes' (77); and the recurring figure of 'Zarathustra's Ape' is later regarded by Nietzsche's protagonist as 'a frothing fool', a kind of false prophet who displays a superficial imitation of his teachings (195). Peter Groff therefore suggests that 'if we take Nietzsche's ostensibly non-hierarchical naturalism at face value, there is at least one respect in which his own writings fall short of this radical vision of nature'. Namely, that he 'consistently and almost systematically disparages what might be seen as the most significant and symbol-laden animal in late nineteenth-century Europe's psychological bestiary' (2004: 18). Perhaps because of its evolutionary proximity to the 'man' that is so often the target of Nietzsche's critique, the ape in *Thus Spoke Zarathustra* can appear, somewhat problematically, to represent a kind of regression.

With these qualifications in mind, it is still fair to say that animals stake significant territory in Nietzsche's philosophical landscape. The use of the terms 'territory' and 'landscape' is quite deliberate here, as the relationship between humans and animals in Nietzsche's text demonstrates an immanent (rather than transcendent) and materialist (rather than idealist) conception of life. That Zarathustra shares the territories he wanders among with animals, even when these animals are sometimes captured within figures of speech, illustrates their importance on both a material and conceptual level. Some critics would point to the examples above as evidence of how Nietzsche has 'perpetuated the old stereotypes of animals and reinforced traditional hierarchical ranking of human beings above animals' (Langer 1999: 90), but such a view misses the nuanced roles animals play in Nietzsche's wide-ranging critique of human arrogance and narcissism. Throughout the text we witness Zarathustra moving 'among men *as* among animals' rather than '*as if* among animals' (2003a: 112); that is, moving a step beyond the figurative imagining of animals discussed in Chapter 1, and towards affirming the shared animality of human and nonhuman.

This shared animality is emphasised when we read that Zarathustra 'speaks of the body . . . insists upon the body' as the site of the 'Ego' (60). In opposition to Descartes, and evoking Spinoza and Leibniz, we read that the 'soul is only a word for something in the body' (61); the soul owes its life to the body and the material world, not to a transcendent power:

Ever more honestly it learns to speak, the Ego: and the more it learns, the more it finds titles and honours for the body and the earth.

My Ego taught me a new pride, I teach it to men: No longer to bury the head in the sand of heavenly things, but to carry it freely, an earthly head which creates meaning for the earth! (60)

This passage affirms the human's embodied relation to the earth. The sickly for Nietzsche are people still bound to the idea of a transcendent god; the healthy are those who affirm materiality and the immanence of life. In *The Antichrist* he critiques 'the vanity that man is the great secret objective of animal evolution', and, on the contrary, asserts that 'man is absolutely not the crown of creation; every creature stands beside him at the same stage of perfection'. For Nietzsche, the human is far from the pinnacle of evolution. If there is any hierarchy in nature then it is 'man' who is relegated to a lower status: 'man is, relatively speaking, the most unsuccessful animal, the sickliest, the one most dangerously strayed from its instincts' (2003b: 136). In *Thus Spoke Zarathustra*, Nietzsche differentiates between 'the poets [who] always think that nature herself is in love with them', the poets who enter a transcendent 'cloudland', and Zarathustra who is 'weary . . . of all the unattainable that is supposed to be reality' (2003a: 150). Zarathustra affirms the importance of thinking in depths rather than heights.

love your depths (rather than your heights)

Overcoming the Human

Nietzsche's protagonist continually speaks to, about and with animals in *Thus Spoke Zarathustra*. In doing so Zarathustra presents a pivotal feature of Nietzsche's philosophy, whereby the immanence of being finds its perfect expression in the animality of the human. This is most powerfully evident in the figure the 'Superman' – a term that has been translated variously as 'Superhuman', 'Overman' and 'Overhuman'. Despite the connotations of the prefix 'Super' in the most common translation of the term, it is important to remember that the 'Superman' doesn't stand for a teleological advancement (or strengthening) of the human but instead points to its *overcoming* of itself (2003a: 41). This overcoming does not, however, mark a shift into some transcendent realm: 'The Superman is the meaning of the earth . . . I entreat you, my brothers, remain true to the earth, and do not believe those who speak to you of superterrestrial hopes! They are prisoners, whether they know it or not' (42). To overcome the human is to see beyond a theological view of the human created by a transcendent force. As such, the Superman is defined by 'openness to the animality of the human being' (Lemm 2009: 5).

Where precisely do animals fit into this project of the Superman, or the overcoming of the human? In the opening pages, Zarathustra does appear to imagine a kind of evolutionary advancement between the animals and the Superman. The latter has already made its way 'from worm to man' and is therefore conceived as the next step in a progression from animals to man: 'All creatures hitherto have created something beyond themselves: and do you want to be the ebb of this great tide, and return to the animals rather than overcome man?' (Nietzsche 2003a: 41). And yet, this evolutionary discourse is one aspect that changes throughout the course of Zarathustra's journey in the book. Towards the end it is precisely the affirmation of the animality of the human that distinguishes the Superman from the so-called 'Higher Men' (note again the 'Super' here is the opposite of the 'Higher') who are the guardians of a joyless reason and morality: 'You Higher Men, the worst about you is: none of you has learned to dance as a man ought to dance – to dance beyond yourselves! . . . *learn* to laugh beyond yourselves!' (306). It is in opposition to the Higher men that Zarathustra moves closer to animality: '"Only now do I know and feel how I love you, my animals".' Zarathustra chooses to enter the nonhuman landscape, 'for the air here outside was better than with the Higher Men' (307). It is in the company of animals that the human – and the rigid ontological categorisation that determines who is worthy of reason and morality – can be overcome.

'The Voluntary Beggar' is perhaps the most revealing section of *Thus Spoke Zarathustra* in presenting how fundamental a (re)discovery of the animality of the human is for the Superman. Taking place just after we have once again been reminded that man 'is something that must be overcome' (279), it becomes clear in this section that to 'dance beyond' the human is to enter into a zone of proximity, both materially and conceptually, with animals. In particular, cows play an important role here, where in their company Zarathustra grows 'warmer and more cheerful' as their 'warm breath touches [his] soul'. But the cows are less interested in Zarathustra than they appear to be in the beggar who is seated 'on the ground . . . persuading the animals to have no fear of him' (280). The beggar reveals that he seeks 'happiness on earth' and believes he can learn this from this bovine encounter:

'I may learn from these cows. For, let me tell you, I have already been talking to them half a morning and they were just about to reply to me. Why do you disturb them?

'If we do not alter and become as cows, we shall not enter into the kingdom of heaven. For there is one thing we should learn from them: rumination.

'And truly, if a man should gain the whole world and not learn this one thing, rumination: what would it profit him! He would not be free from his affliction . . . regard these cows!' (280)

These cows are not simply stand-ins for a human quality; rather, they possess an *animal* quality that humans must engage. This is reinforced by the fact that the cows are then comically indifferent to the heated discussion between Zarathustra and the beggar. Antoine Traisnel – who wittily calls *Thus Spoke Zarathustra*, given its numerous animal figures, Nietzsche's 'philosafari' – argues that 'The Voluntary Beggar' highlights 'the uncanniness of the quasi-encounter between thinkers who use cows as models of wisdom and "real" cows standing before them, amazed, rendered speechless, so to speak, by what they see.' To be sure, it is laughable that the human could ever be *the same* as the cow, equated naively with the cow's being in some 'ideal interspecies synthesis' (Traisnel 2012: 91–2). The serious point is that the cows' rumination expresses a specifically bovine form of culture and one from which humans can learn.

Thus Spoke Animality

It is not just quiet, ruminating animals that enter a significant territory in *Thus Spoke Zarathustra*. Nietzsche also experiments with animal voice. This is evident in 'The Convalescent', when Zarathustra urges the animals to '"go on talking and let me listen! Your talking is such refreshment"':

'Oh Zarathustra,' said the animals then, 'all things themselves dance for such as think as we: they come and offer their hand and laugh and flee – and return.

'Everything goes, everything returns; the wheel of existence rolls for ever. Everything dies, everything blossoms anew; the year of existence runs on for ever.

'Everything breaks, everything is joined anew; the same house of existence builds itself for ever. Everything departs, everything meets again; the ring of existence if true to itself for ever.

'Existence begins in every instant; the ball There rolls around every Here. The middle is everywhere. The path of eternity is crooked.' (2003a: 234)

Rejecting teleology – whether the kind associated with Judeo-Christian religion or with Darwinian evolution – the animals espouse a cyclical 'dance' of existence. They do so by speaking directly *to* Zarathustra, and even go on to speak *for* him:

'And if you should die now, O Zarathustra: behold, we know too what you would then say to yourself – but your animals ask you not to die yet!
[...]
'"Now I die and decay," you would say, "and in an instant I shall be nothingness. Souls are as mortal as bodies.

'"But the complex of causes in which I am entangled will recur – it will create me again! I myself am part of these causes of the eternal recurrence.

'"I shall return, with this sun, with this earth, with this eagle, with this serpent – *not* to a new life or a better life or a similar life:

'"I shall return eternally to this identical and self-same life, in the greatest things and in the smallest, to teach once more the eternal recurrence of all things"' (237)

Here the animals present a theory of 'eternal recurrence', sometimes translated as 'eternal return', which expresses neither a scientific view of time nor a spiritual immortality. Rather, the idea of the eternal recurrence is posed as a kind of challenge to test who could bear the weight of it, which elsewhere Nietzsche calls the 'heaviest burden' (2006: 152). In other words, the true affirmation of life would be in coming to terms with a notion that all that has gone before, both painful and pleasurable experience, will be repeated eternally. We are not asked to affirm the eternal recurrence as factual truth, or to morally approve of all that has happened; instead, it is presented to raise the existential question of how we would respond to this call to affirm the eternal return of all things. Lawrence Hatab illuminates this existential call in his book *Nietzsche's Life Sentences*, arguing that although not an 'objective, scientific, cosmological fact', there is a 'literal' dimension to the eternal recurrence that makes it 'more than simply a hypothetical thought experiment pertaining only to human psychology; he always took it to express something about life and the world as such' (Hatab 2005: 8–9). In espousing the theory of eternal recurrence, the animals are included not simply in a symbolic or psychological appropriation by the human, but as part of a literal affirmation of that which is outside the human.

In announcing the theory of eternal recurrence, the animals in *Thus Spoke Zarathustra* play an active role in Nietzsche's cultivation of non-anthropocentric thought. In a sense they are anthropomorphised creatures who clearly speak in the language of humans. But unlike the psychoanalytic animals discussed in Chapter 1, which are anthropomorphised to confirm their role in the symbolic order, Nietzsche's animals are anthropomorphised to non-anthropocentric ends. That is, the deeper *concept* they are communicating is one that brings human and nonhuman into closer ontological proximity. Following Traisnel, we can think of Zarathustra's relation to the animals – because and not in spite of their 'figurative baggage' – as part of an 'allegorical distance' created by Nietzsche which is 'necessary in order to unsettle both a strictly figurative viewpoint *and* a naturalist perspective on animal life' (2012: 87). Influenced by Walter Benjamin's theory of the 'remedial potential of allegory', Traisnel argues that *Thus Spoke Zarathustra* allows for a distance to be kept between human and animal without erasing the animal entirely. In other words, figurative animals allow the necessary distance to maintain *difference*, to not simply equate human and animal in a naive continuity or 'the dream of a perfect epistemic comprehension of nature', while also challenging the notions of opposition and hierarchy between human and animal: 'the distinction between men and animals is maintained throughout *Zarathustra*, only this distinction is neither unconditional nor transhistorical. And it is certainly *not natural*' (2012: 87; 96; 90). This reading would also allow for a more nuanced view of the above mentioned camels, lions and snakes who appeared to be simply figurative substitutes for human emotions and attributes. We might say that when Nietzsche gives Zarathustra's animals the speech and characteristics of humans he does so not as an erasure of animality, nor as a homogenisation of animals, but as an affirmation of how animals play their part in theorising the human's animality.

Thus Spoke Zarathustra ends by affirming the voice of animality with the language of humanity. In the final section, 'The Sign', that voice speaks many voices, for both Zarathustra and his animals, and articulates their ontological entanglement. Zarathustra declares that it is the animals and not the Higher Men that are his 'rightful companions' (2003a: 333):

Thus spoke Zarathustra; then, however, he suddenly heard that he was surrounded by countless birds, swarming and fluttering – the whirring of so many wings and the throng about his head, however, were so great that he shut his eyes . . . as he was clutching about, above and underneath himself, warding off the tender birds, behold, then something even stranger occurred: for in doing so he clutched unawares a thick, warm mane of hair; at the same time, however, a roar rang out in front of him – the gentle, protracted roar of a lion.

'*The sign has come,*' said Zarathustra, and his heart was transformed. And in truth, when it grew clear before him, there lay at his feet a sallow, powerful animal that lovingly pressed its head against his knee and would not leave him, behaving like a dog that has found his old master again. The doves, however, were no less eager than the lion with their love; and every time a dove glided across the lion's nose, the lion shook its head and wondered and laughed . . . [and] continually licked the tears that fell down upon Zarathustra's hands, roaring and growling shyly as he did so. Thus did these animals. (334–5)

In this striking passage the multiplicity of animality is heard; Zarathustra's speech is displaced by the sounds of birds 'swarming and fluttering', and a lion paradoxically 'roaring and growling shyly'. This is in stark contrast to the Higher Men who, at the sound of the lion, 'all cried out as with a *single* throat and fled back and in an instant had vanished' (335; italics mine). The territory staked by animals in *Thus Spoke Zarathustra* is heterogeneous, lively and full, whereas the believers in civilisation scatter as a homogenised, stolid group into emptiness. 'Thus spoke Zarathustra' becomes 'Thus did these animals'; if we spent less time elevating human speech to a transcendent sphere of truth, we would have more time to listen to the earthly call of animality.

BECOMING ANIMAL

In *Nietzsche and Philosophy*, first published in French in 1962, Gilles Deleuze describes how Nietzsche's 'affirmative animal[s]' are linked to a philosophy of 'becoming' (2006: 161). The Higher Men in *Thus Spoke Zarathustra* are constricted by their faith in rigid categories of human and animal being, whereas Zarathustra's animals enact more fluid and transformative encounters. Central to Deleuze's reading of Nietzsche's animals is the idea that they help to express a non-dialectical philosophy. Dialectical thought seeks to overcome oppositions (thesis and antithesis) by resolving them (synthesis), but this problematically elevates the 'power of the negative as a theoretical principle manifested in opposition and contradiction' (184). The dialectic, as Deleuze writes elsewhere, is a 'false movement' because it takes contradiction as its starting point: 'the concrete will never be attained by combining the inadequacy of one concept with the inadequacy of its opposite. The singular will never be attained by correcting a generality with another generality' (1991: 44). The potential this critique of dialectics holds for animal theorists is found in its shift away from preconceived divides between generalised abstract categories, such as 'animal' and 'human', and in its resistance to any ideal synthesis between them. Deleuze finds in Nietzsche an ally in his efforts to theorise the multiple modes of animality shared between, and transformed by, non/human encounters. Following Nietzsche, in Deleuze's philosophy, including in his collaborations with the radical psychoanalyst Félix Guattari, there is a link between affirmative animality and a creative becoming.

Affect Animals

In the influential tenth chapter of their 1980 book *A Thousand Plateaus*, Deleuze and Guattari outline three different ways in which we can distinguish animals. First, there are the 'Oedipal animals . . . "my" cat, "my" dog'. These are the animals, often family pets, which are sentimentalised and 'individuated' as little humans. The fact that they are termed 'Oedipal' animals points to Deleuze and Guattari's distaste for the ways in which psychoanalysis reduces animals to stand-ins for human figures in a familial drama (as detailed in Chapter 1). When psychoanalysis pays attentions to such animals it is simply 'to discover a daddy, a mommy, a little brother behind them'. The second kind of animals outlined by Deleuze and Guattari are the 'classification, or State animals', those with 'characteristics or attributes' that shape them as 'archetypes' and 'models' or fit them into 'divine myths'. These animals might include the symbolic beasts in religions or tied to national identities, as well as other allegorical creatures used to tell human stories. The crucial point about these first two kinds of animals is that they are seen as stand-ins for a seemingly higher human concern; they are anthropomorphised creatures and they serve anthropocentric ends. The third kind of animals that Deleuze and Guattari point to are the more nomadic 'pack or affect animals that form a multiplicity, a becoming', rather than containing a unified, fixed being (2004: 265). It is this third way of approaching animals that takes into account their own material, affective qualities that refuses to assimilate them into an anthropocentric and anthropomorphic arrangement. It is 'affect animals' that we encounter when the stable category of the human subject is uprooted, when the animality of the human is affirmed, and when the human forms an affinity with the animal.

The emphasis Deleuze and Guattari place on affect animals as 'pack' animals is not meant as a comment on the fact 'that certain animals live in packs' or such 'evolutionary classifications': 'What we are saying is that every animal is fundamentally a band, a pack. That it has pack modes, rather than characteristics, even if further distinctions within these modes are called for.' 'We do not become animal', they add, 'without a fascination for the pack, for multiplicity' (264). Deleuze and Guattari are here influenced by fellow French philosopher Henri Bergson. At the beginning of the twentieth century, and in the wake of Darwinism, Bergson's *Creative Evolution* sought to move from a discussion of the quantitative classification of animals to an exploration of their qualitative differences:

> There is no manifestation of life which does not contain, in a rudimentary state – either latent or potential, – the essential characters of most other manifestations. The difference is in the proportions . . . *the group must not be defined by the possession of certain characters, but by its tendency to emphasize them.* (Bergson 1998: 106)

What Deleuze and Guattari describe as thinking in 'modes' rather than 'characteristics' can be thought of along similar lines to Bergson's assertion that he is concerned with qualitative 'tendencies' rather than quantitative 'states' (1998: 106). Following Bergson, Deleuze and Guattari present their own neo-evolutionism, which takes issue with an understanding of 'evolution' as signalling a process towards a more distinct organism or perfectly differentiated category of being, and instead emphasises 'involution' as the term which best captures the symbiotic but never fixed relations between different animal worlds or milieus. Deleuze and Guattari's philosophy of 'becoming' is concerned with *involving* rather than *evolving*, with 'alliance' and 'transversal communications' rather than 'descent and filiation' (2004: 263). We are offered a horizontal view of animals in their heterogeneous environments where the focus is on functions and affects rather than forms and characteristics.

Deleuze and Guattari's conceptualisation of 'becoming-animal' accounts for intensive, affective encounters between human and nonhuman. In rejecting 'majoritarian' modes of thought, which are 'constant and homogeneous', becoming-animal signals a process of 'minoritarian' potential and creativity. To truly encounter affect animals is to enter a zone of proximity and indiscernibility with animality, to be open and responsive to the 'becomings-animal traversing human beings and sweeping them away, affecting the animal no less than the human' (261). Crucially, becoming-animal is not about identification with animals, nor is it a matter of imitating animal forms or behaviours – it is not to act *like* an animal. Most important of all, 'becoming does not occur in the imagination . . . Becomings-animal are neither dreams nor phantasies' (262). Instead, becoming is about reconfiguring our conception of material reality, for becomings are, above all, 'perfectly real'; what we have to determine is 'which reality is at issue here?':

it is clear that the human being does not 'really' become an animal any more than the animal 'really' becomes something else. Becoming produces nothing other than itself. We fall into a false alternative if we say that you either imitate or you are. What is real is the becoming itself, the block of becoming, not the supposedly fixed terms through which that which becomes passes . . . becoming lacks a subject distinct from itself. (262)

Rather than describing a movement from one type of being (human) to another (animal), Deleuze and Guattari seek to challenge the ontological foundations on which we divide being into such categories and then conceive of relations between them. They are less interested in claiming subjectivity for individual animals than with uprooting the very notion of fixed and stable subjects. When entering a human-animal relation we don't travel from animal to human (or vice versa) but are always 'between', always in 'the middle': 'a line of becoming has neither beginning nor end, departure nor arrival, origin nor destination . . . becoming is neither one nor two, nor the relation of the two; it is the in-between, the border or line of flight or descent running perpendicular to both' (323). As Zarathustra's animals say: 'The middle is everywhere' (Nietzsche 2003a: 234).

In *Kafka: Toward a Minor Literature*, Deleuze and Guattari expand on what it means to become animal by focusing on Franz Kafka's literary animals:

There is no longer man or animal, since each deterritorializes the other, in a conjunction of flux, in a continuum of reversible intensities. Instead, it is now a question of becoming that includes the maximum of difference as a difference of intensity, the crossing of a barrier, a rising or a falling, a bending or an erecting . . . there is a circuit of states that forms a mutual becoming, in the heart of a necessarily multiple or collective assemblage. (1986: 22)

Deleuze and Guattari's vocabulary – of conjunctions, continuums, circuits, and of intensity, mutuality, multiplicity – expresses the intimate and non-dialectical process of becoming-animal. It 'is a creative line of escape that says nothing other than what it is . . . a unique method that replaces subjectivity' (36). Exploring territories of indeterminacy between human and animal, Deleuze and Guattari theorise a shared event of becoming different, of becoming entangled with otherness in a de- and then re-making of ontological boundaries.

Deleuze and Guattari therefore provide a rigorously non-anthropocentric way to think not only about the animality of the human, but also the animality of the animal. That they do so by unsettling oppositional and hierarchical categories means that it would be a mistake to see their three types of animals as themselves fixed to particular species. Affect animals don't form an exclusive group as any animal can 'be treated in all three ways':

> There is always the possibility that a given animal, a louse, a cheetah or an elephant, will be treated as a pet, my little beast. And at the other extreme, it is also possible for any animal to be treated in the mode of the pack or swarm; . . . Even the cat, even the dog. (2004: 266)

Wild or domesticated, large or small, Deleuze and Guattari carefully avoid falling into the trap of linking specific animals irrevocably to specific categories. In doing so they offer one of most inventive examples in western philosophy of an animal ontology that critiques both anthropocentric and anthropomorphic uses of animals at the same time as conceptualising 'lines of flight' (262) from such anthropomorphic conceptualisations and anthropocentric arrangements.

Becoming without Animals

Deleuze and Guattari's conceptualisation of 'becoming-animal' is not without limitations. Even the most faithful of Deleuzo-Guattarian theorists would have to concede that their writings don't expand in detail on the actual experiences of individual animals or their widespread (mis)treatment. This concession is evident among critics working across a range of disciplines. For example, at the same time as arguing for the use of Deleuze and Guattari in discussions of animal ethics, Lori Brown has noted that in emphasising becoming-animal as a means of 'challenging and breaking up various human institutions' they fail to 'address institutions that have a negative impact on other animals' – that is, most of their examples of becomings-animal are concerned with what takes place in 'mental illness, in music and other art forms, in tales of wild men, vampires and werewolves' (Brown 2007: 262). Similarly, when discussing their importance to considerations of animals in art, Steve Baker has written that 'animals, for Deleuze and Guattari, seem to operate more as a device of writing . . . than as living beings whose conditions of life were of direct concern to the writers' (Baker 2002: 95). These limitations of Deleuze and Guattari's approach to animals open on to wider concerns about the role of animal ontology. For example, we could question whether Nietzsche's *Thus Spoke Zarathustra* demonstrates concern for specific 'institutions that have a negative impact' on animals or indeed the everyday 'conditions of life' of animals.

It is for this reason that some contemporary animal theorists have been sceptical about the value of Deleuze and Guattari's approach to animality. The boldest critique is found in *When Species Meet*, where Donna Haraway is emphatic in her dislike of 'becoming-animal', and of Deleuze and Guattari's conceptualisation of animality in *A Thousand Plateaus* more broadly:

> I want to understand why Deleuze and Guattari here leave me so angry when what we want seems so similar. Despite much that I love in other work of Deleuze, here I find little but the two writers' scorn for all that is mundane and ordinary and the profound absence of curiosity about or respect for and with actual animals . . . No earthly animal would look twice at these authors, at least not in their textual garb in this chapter. (2008: 28)

Despite seeming alliances between them – and Haraway notes, albeit hidden away at the end of a scathing footnote, 'of course, I am indebted to Deleuze and Guattari, among others, for my ability to think in "assemblages"' (314) – she argues that they don't pay enough attention to ordinary animals and that their animal theorising is, as a result, 'of the sublime, not the earthly, not the mud'. She goes on to accuse Deleuze and Guattari's becoming-animal of demonstrating one of the clearest displays in all philosophy of 'incuriosity about animals, and horror at the ordinariness of flesh' (27–30).

What Haraway's lively critique of Deleuze and Guattari appears to overlook, however, is that the comment she finds most distasteful – '*anyone who likes cats or dogs is a fool*' – occurs only when they are outlining the Oedipalisation of animals which 'draws us into a narcissistic contemplation' and reinforces the tendency for anthropomorphism (Deleuze and Guattari 2004: 265). Their point is not that we should care less for cats and dogs, but that we shouldn't always already place cats and dogs within our invented schemas, and that we shouldn't presume to *know* cats and dogs: 'if such encounters and becomings-animal are to be truly transformational, they must proceed in such a way that animals are not approached in familiar, anthropomorphic terms' (Calarco 2008: 42). Lifting Deleuze and Guattari's (admittedly startling) statement out of context, Haraway risks giving the impression that they are cruelly dismissive of all animals, when in fact they are exposing the ways in which certain animals have been reduced to mere psychoanalytic facades with 'a daddy, a mommy, a little brother behind them' (2004: 265–6); they are attempting to unsettle and complicate our conceptualisation of human/animal relations by *including* non-human animals in their wider ontological and ethical project. How much we like our pets is not necessarily the best measure of how much we escape binary conceptualisations of human and animal, nor of how ethical our treatment of animals is, as will be considered in Chapter 3. Yet, to provide some balance to Haraway's view of how Deleuze and Guattari think about owners and their pets we can turn to an interview Deleuze gave towards the end of his life when he clarified that 'generally people who like animals don't have a human relationship with animals, they have an *animal* relationship with the animal, and that's quite beautiful' (Deleuze and Parnet 2012; italics mine). To have an animal relationship with an animal is precisely what Deleuze and Guattari mean by becoming-animal.

Deleuze's own writings about animals, aside from his collaborations with Guattari, are also important to consider. In response to Haraway's accusation of their 'horror at the ordinariness of flesh', we could turn to a passage from his 1981 study *Francis Bacon: The Logic of Sensation*:

> meat is not dead flesh; it retains all the sufferings and assumes all the colours of living flesh. It manifests such convulsive pain and vulnerability, but also such delightful invention, colour, acrobatics. Bacon does not say, 'Pity the beasts', but rather that every man who suffers is a piece of meat. Meat is the common zone of man and the beast, their zone of indiscernibility. (2005: 17)

Here Deleuze brings the aliveness of flesh into a zone of proximity between human and beast that ruptures distinctions between them. Of course we could say that this is another example of focusing on artistic rather than real animals, but to do so would be to accept the implication that art is necessarily unable to *express* any kind of reality – a claim that would be rather impoverished in consigning all visual, literary and, for that matter, philosophical works merely to failed representations. The power of Bacon's paintings for Deleuze is that they express 'the reality of becoming' which is 'a zone of indiscernibility more profound than any sentimental identification: the man who suffers is a beast, the beast who suffers is a man' (18). This zone of indiscernibility is not an erasure of difference so that the human and animal resemble each other and become the same, but rather an intensive multiplication of differences (including of different animalities) that render oppositional categories of 'same' and 'different' defunct. Like Kafka's literature, Bacon's paintings express an imperceptible ontological reality, where the materials that make up human and animal are shared in all their differences. Encounters with animals, whether in life or in the artistic expressions of life, serve to spark in us an affective response: 'What revolutionary person', asks Deleuze, 'in art, politics, religion, or elsewhere – has not felt that extreme moment when he or she was nothing but a beast, and became responsible not for the calves that died, but *before* the calves that died?' We are reminded in such moments that 'animals are part of humanity' and that 'we are all cattle' (18). There may be an 'absence of curiosity' about 'actual animals', as Haraway suggests, but in its place what characterises the Deleuzian view of animality is 'fascination' (Deleuze and Guattari 2004: 264; Lawlor 2008: 176). The point is not that Deleuze and Guattari are incurious about animals but that they are *more* than curious.

Becoming with Animals

Haraway's dismissal of Deleuze and Guattari does raise significant questions about who or what animal theory is *about* and who or what it is written *for*. If animals are to be subjected to theoretical enquiry that is to be read by humans, how important is it to accurately represent the individual lives of these animals? One limitation of 'becoming-animal' is the repeated appearance of the singular 'animal' and the way it is used to describe a process that is seemingly open to all animals. While this allows Deleuze and Guattari to open up their concept to all kinds of creatures while avoiding essentialist species identities, it can leave the impression that each animal could easily be substituted for another. Even if this inattention to individual animals is not sufficiently problematic to entirely undermine their non-anthropocentric and non-anthropomorphic ontological project, it does leave us wondering whether we might, in fact, need various different conceptualisations of 'becoming' for such a vast array of animals.

In order to account for individually and historically locatable animal encounters, Haraway's theoretical approach differs from Deleuze and Guattari's in that she explicitly draws on her own everyday personal encounters with animals in order to open onto wider contexts. However, in turning to think about Haraway's formulation of becoming, what she calls 'becoming with', it would be unhelpful to view this concept in opposition to Deleuzian 'becoming'. For as Rosi Braidotti has convincingly argued, in an article which appeared the year before *When Species Meet*, Haraway and Deleuze actually display a deep 'alliance' in presenting theories which are 'materialist' and 'neo-literal', and therefore not limited to the 'textual' and 'resolutely not metaphorical': 'Haraway shares with Deleuze two key features: serious neo-foundational materialism on the one hand and a rigorous theory of relationality on the other' (2006: 200). Indeed, Haraway's problems with Deleuze and Guattari seem to stem more from her dislike of their *style of* theorising than from their ontology. Where animal theory is concerned, it is more helpful to see Deleuze and Haraway in a productive, if uneasy, alliance.

The Companion Species Manifesto and *When Species Meet* are filled with stories of 'becoming with' animals. The singularity of each animal and their situated role in the world is vitally important for Haraway, where her discussion allows readers to 'meet cloned dogs, databased tigers, a baseball writer on crutches [her father], a health and genetics activist in Fresno, wolves and dogs in Syria and the French Alps' as well as 'tsetse flies and guinea pigs in a Zimbabwean lab in a young adult novel, feral cats, whales wearing cameras, felons and pooches in training in prison' and, central to her project, 'a talented dog and middle-aged woman playing a sport together in California' (2008: 5). The latter refers to Haraway and her Australian Shepherd Cayenne, who is cast in a starring role in both books, as seen below and in Chapter 3. Haraway's 'becoming with' therefore elaborates on how 'ordinary multispecies' are part of a 'naturalcultural' framework of becoming, located variously in 'house, lab, field, zoo, park, office, prison, ocean, stadium, barn, or factory' (2008: 3–5). Influenced by French sociologist and anthropologist Bruno Latour's argument that 'Nature and Society are not two distinct poles, but one and the same production of successive states of societies-nature, of collectives' (1993: 139), Haraway emphasises the non-hierarchical and non-oppositional relations between human and nonhuman, culture and nature: 'conceiving of "nature" and "culture" as either polar opposites or universal categories is foolish . . . Instead of opposites, we get the whole sketchpad of the modern geometrician's fevered brain with which to draw relationality' (2003: 8). For Haraway, ontology should never allow for one species or category of being to have control over another; the foundation of being consists in multiple stories of cross-species entanglements: 'companion species' is 'less a category than a pointer to an ongoing "becoming with"' (2008: 16–17). Claiming to be a 'creature' and philosopher 'of the mud' (2; 28), Haraway provides an 'ontological choreography' (2003: 100; 2008: 67) consisting of a 'multipartner mud dance' where 'the partners do not precede their relating; all that is, is the fruit of becoming with: those are the mantras of companion species' (2008: 16). Echoing Deleuze and Guattari's 'rhizome' concept, which emphasises horizontal growth rather than the hierarchical verticality of 'arborescent' systems (2004: 7–8), Haraway writes that 'the shape of my kin networks looks more like a trellis or an esplanade than a tree. You can't tell up from down, and everything seems to go sidewise.' 'Becoming with' is an everyday enacting of 'multidirectional gene flow', of 'multidirectional flows of bodies and values' that 'is and has always been the name of the game of life on earth' (2003: 9)

Becoming *with* places emphasis, then, on the genetic and emotional intimacy of embodied relations. This is evident from the beginning of *When Species Meet*, which opens with the tantalising question: 'Whom and what do I touch when I touch my dog?' (3). *The Companion Species Manifesto* also commences with discussion of Haraway's Australian Shepherd, Cayenne. It all started with a kiss:

> Ms Cayenne Pepper continues to colonize all my cells . . . I bet if you checked our DNA, you'd find some potent transfections between us. Her saliva must have the viral vectors. Surely, her darter-tongue kisses have been irresistible . . . I'm sure our genomes are more alike than they should be. There must be some molecular record of our touch in the codes of living that will leave traces in the world . . . Her red merle Australian Shepherd's quick and lithe tongue has swabbed the tissues of my tonsils, with all their eager immune system receptors . . . We have

had forbidden conversation; we have had oral intercourse; we are bound in telling story upon story with nothing but the facts. We are training each other in acts of communication we barely understand. We are, constitutively, companion species. We make each other up, in the flesh. (2003: 1–3; original in italics)

In this remarkable passage – with its emphasis on transfections, viral vectors, and darter-tongue kisses – Haraway brings woman and dog, human and Australian Shepherd, into a messy, impure materialist alliance. 'Inter-species kisses have the potential', Lynn Turner argues in 'When Species Kiss', 'to disrupt species boundaries': each kiss 'solicits an undecidability into the divisions between subjects and species once thought to be decisive' (2010: 63). Instead of dividing animal from human based on their different access to language, their interspecies 'oral intercourse' signals a meaning-making and world-making encounter of its own.

That a *kiss* should spark this challenge to the divide between humans and animals is telling given that it involves an embodied communication that depends upon those very tissues and organs used to produce speech. In contrast to Lacan's encounter with his dog in Chapter 1, where human speech is used to bring the animal 'to order', Haraway's seductive theorising foregrounds the non-linguistic ways in which species become materially and significantly entangled. What such encounters present are 'figures', 'material-semiotic nodes or knots in which diverse bodies and meanings co-shape one another' to create 'creatures of imagined possibility and creatures of fierce and ordinary reality' (2008: 4). Rather than holding an *a priori* identity, human and nonhuman co-shape one another as part of an intimate entanglement of agency whereby they continually 'make each other up, in the flesh'. Such a conceptualisation of multispecies figures offers us a way to think about companion species entanglements that sits well alongside Haraway's exploration of cyborgs and primates in earlier texts, including *Primate Vision* and *Simians, Cyborgs and Woman*, which remain important for animal theorists. After all, in her 'Cyborg Manifesto', first published in 1985 and later collected in *Simians, Cyborgs and Women*, the human/animal divide is central to Haraway's concerns. It is the first of three 'crucial boundary breakdowns' (the second is 'organism and machine' and the third is 'physical and non-physical'):

language, tool use, social behaviour, mental events, nothing really convincingly settles the separation of human and animal. And many people no longer feel the need of such a separation; indeed, many branches of feminist culture affirm the pleasure of connection of human and other living creatures. Movements for animal rights are not irrational denials of human uniqueness; they are clear-sighted recognition of connection across the discredited breach of nature and culture. (1991: 151)

Reading about Haraway's multivalent figures that transform ontological boundaries also provides an impetus to return afresh to Zarathustra's apes, snakes, lions and birds as well as Deleuzian cats, dogs and fleshy cattle. All of these meaning-making creatures signal an important shift away from a privileging of human being over animal being, instead showing how humanity is intimately bound together with animality. Nietzsche, Deleuze and Haraway all provide a meaningful materialist territory in which species can meet.

POSTHUMAN ANIMALS

The ontological entanglements that we find in the writings of Nietzsche, Deleuze and Haraway speak in different ways to a growing interest in contemporary theory with what has become known as 'posthumanism'. The prefix 'post' in this term, in a similar manner to Nietzsche's 'Super' in the 'Superman', often creates the misconception that it bypasses a concern with humanity and celebrates an imagined future in which human beings will become disembodied. This might explain why Haraway, for example, distances herself from the term (2008: 19). But, as Katherine Hayles notes in *How We Became Posthuman*, 'the posthuman does not really mean the end of humanity. It signals the end of a certain conception of the human' (1999: 287). An important distinction also needs to be drawn between posthumanism and transhumanism, whereby the latter can be seen to fantasise about the engineering of an enhanced human form. Point 7 of the 2012 'Transhumanist Declaration' does list 'non-human animals' among beings that deserve moral consideration (alongside not only humans but also 'any future artificial intellects, modified life forms, or other intelligences to which technological and scientific advance may give rise'). Yet it is clear that the transhumanists present a primarily human-centred techno-scientific vision, as point 1 of the 'Declaration' makes clear: 'Humanity stands to be profoundly affected by science and technology in the future. We envision the possibility of broadening human potential by overcoming aging, cognitive shortcomings, involuntary suffering' and even, the authors add, 'our confinement to planet Earth' (More and Vita-More 2013: 54). As Max More outlines, transhumanism places its faith in 'taking personal charge of creating better futures' and continual 'progress' via 'reason, technology, scientific method, and human creativity' (4). To confuse matters, transhumanists often use the term 'posthuman' to describe this future vision for humanity: 'Becoming posthuman means exceeding the limitations that define the less desirable aspects of the "human condition."' Posthuman beings would, for the transhumanists, be freed from 'disease, aging, and inevitable death' and 'space colonization and the creation of rich virtual worlds' are actions that might help achieve this (4). The important point is that where transhumanism seemingly wills the engineering of a super-enhanced humanity and desires an anthropocentric world for the future, posthumanism attends to ontological entanglements between human bodies and nonhuman animals, and opens up non-anthropocentric worldviews, *in the present*.

Cary Wolfe stresses the distinction between posthumanism and transhumanism in *What is Posthumanism?* They are, in fact, 'opposite' theoretical approaches because posthumanism critiques humanism whereas 'transhumanism should be seen as an *intensification* of humanism' (2010: xv). Posthumanism is still concerned with humanity, but it takes a critical stance towards humanism; it urges humans to respect and respond to nonhuman worlds, and to reject essentialist and hierarchical divisions between culture and nature. This in turn also enables us, as Wolfe illustrates, 'to describe the human and its characteristic modes of communication, interaction, meaning, social significations, and affective investments with *greater* specificity once we have removed meaning from the ontologically closed domain of consciousness, reason, reflection' (xxv). The posthumanism that is of importance to animal theory is the version that seeks to move beyond liberal humanist conceptualisations that continually privilege the human and divide humans and animals based on capacities for reason and language. Where transhumanism supports, and indeed depends upon, the human arrogance that has often sidelined thoughts about animals and claimed transcendence over animality, posthumanist theory shares an affinity with animal theory in the sense of seeking to uproot the privileged position of human individualism in anthropocentric arrangements of everyday life and thought.

Speciesism and the Subject of Politics

In his groundbreaking book, *Animal Rites: American Culture, the Discourse of Species, and Posthumanist Theory*, Wolfe demonstrates that to adopt a posthumanist approach to animals is to address the 'unexamined framework of *speciesism*' (2003b: 1) – a term originally coined by activist Richard Ryder in the early 1970s and discussed in relation to ethics in Chapter 4. While the discipline of cultural studies has, over the past few decades, offered sophisticated critiques of racial, class, gender and sexual prejudices, these critiques have failed to address an underlying human bias at the heart of our cultural analysis. This, according to Wolfe, signals 'a fundamental repression' in even the most progressive ethical and political projects: the 'question of nonhuman subjectivity' is ignored and it is taken for granted 'that the subject is always already human' (1). Having begun to address racism, classism and (hetero)sexism we might be tempted to think of speciesism as the logical next step. But this would suggest that the prejudices of society – and the critiques offered via various cultural forms, whether in art, literature or philosophy – progress in some kind of linear order. On the contrary, just as analyses of racism, classism and (hetero) sexism are most rigorous when their intersections are accounted for, critiques of speciesism are strongest when combined with critiques of these other ills in society. Indeed, according to Wolfe, posthumanist animal theory has the potential to widely reassess assumptions in all of these other fields of critique, because 'it fundamentally unsettles and reconfigures the question of the knowing subject and the disciplinary paradigms and procedures that take for granted its form and reproduce it' (2010: xxix). Posthumanist animal theorists like Wolfe provide a starting point from which we can assess the relationship between discrimination against species and these other forms of prejudice.

As well as posing a challenge to the knowing subject, and the academic disciplines that revolve around it, posthumanist animal theory also has something important to say about the political subject – that is, about who has political agency and who politics is for. Posthumanism includes animals at the heart of its critique of the politics founded on liberal humanism:

> one of the hallmarks of humanism – and even more specifically that
> kind of humanism called liberalism – is its penchant for that kind
> of pluralism, in which the sphere of attention and consideration
> (intellectual or ethical) is broadened and extended to previously
> marginalized groups, but without in the least destabilizing or throwing
> into radical question the schema of the human who undertakes such
> pluralisation. In that event, pluralism becomes *incorporation*, and the
> projects of humanism (intellectually) and liberalism (politically) are
> extended, and indeed extended in a rather classic sort of way. (Wolfe
> 2010: 99)

Pluralism is an insufficient model to extend intellectual, ethical and political consideration to marginalised humans and animals because it fails to address the structural asymmetries from which those marginalised humans and animals would enter the plurality. If the aim is simply to extend consideration based on the dominant political discourse, then all those entering the political arena will become subjects of that discourse. Posthumanist approaches instead seek to provide the theoretical tools to interrogate the very foundations of this pluralism and expose its flaws and limitations. In so doing, they critique the neoliberal politics of late capitalism.

But posthumanism also poses important questions for other political philosophers who radically oppose neoliberal capitalism. This would include neo-Marxist and neo-Lacanian thinkers, most notably Slavoj Žižek and Alain

Badiou, whose work seeks to recapture the radical potential of the 'subject' in order to counter the neoliberal, postmodernist malaise which precludes any 'rupturing new' socio-political formation (Badiou and Žižek 2009: 58). To be sure, the subject Žižek and Badiou speak of is not, as Calarco notes, the 'autonomous, domineering, atomistic subject of modernity' but 'one who bears and is responsible to an event and alterity that exceeds it' (2008: 12). However, any common ground that might be found with animal theorists seeking to include animals in political thought is difficult to locate because, while they offer a different political subject from metaphysical humanist discourse, 'it is not at all clear that it opens onto something other than metaphysical *anthropocentrism*. When these theorists speak of the subject as being called into being as a response to an event of some sort, it is always a human subject that is being described' and, Calarco adds, 'it is always an *anthropogenic* event that gives rise to the human subject' (12–13). Žižek may in his writings occasionally display some sympathy for 'animals slaughtered for our consumption' (2008: 45), but there is little evidence that this is matched by their inclusion in his political ontology. Such awareness of cruelty towards animals falls some way short of earlier, more polemical, anti-capitalist and anti-humanist critiques of violence against animals, such as from Theodor Adorno and Max Horkheimer, who lament the cruel treatment of 'defenseless animals' from 'nauseating physiological laboratories' to 'arena and slaughterhouse'. The twentieth century, they argue, displays an 'unrelenting exploitation of the animal kingdom' (1997: 245–6).

Where Badiou is concerned, anthropocentrism is evident in his formulation of what qualifies as a political event and who qualifies as a political subject. The true subject of politics is one who *thinks*, and the only capacity for thought is found in the human: in Badiou's *Metapolitics*, for example, political events – the times when 'certain instances of politics have had or will have a relation to truth' – have the common feature of a 'generic humanity of the people engaged in them . . . They bring about a representation of the collective capacity on the basis of a rigorous equality between each of their agents' (2005: 97). 'Equality' here is defined on human terms:

> Equality means that the political actor is represented under the sole
> sign of the uniquely human capacity. Interest is not a uniquely human
> capacity. All living things have as their imperative for survival the
> pursuit of their own interests. Thought is the one and only uniquely
> human capacity, and thought, strictly speaking, is simply that through
> which the human animal is seized and traversed by the trajectory of
> truth. Thus, a politics worthy of being interrogated by philosophy
> under the idea of justice is one whose unique general axiom is: people
> think, people are capable of truth. (97–8)

The implication of this statement is that the living thing that is not human is therefore relegated to an instinct for survival, a selfishness which pursues its own instincts and interests. In *The Communist Hypothesis*, Badiou's conceptualisation of animality is almost the exact reverse of Nietzsche's: the bounds of individualism – 'selfishness', 'competition', 'finitude' – are 'one and the same thing' as the bounds of 'animality' which need to be overcome (2010: 234).

In *The Century*, animals also appear to have little to do with Badiou's political ontology. After the two dominant modes of thought about 'man' in the post-Nietzschean, post-god twentieth century – namely radical humanism (exemplified by Jean-Paul Sartre) and radical anti-humanism (exemplified by Michel Foucault) – Badiou laments this turning of 'man' into 'animal' brought about by a move towards what he sees as a politically flaccid concern with species extinction, ecology and bioethics: 'We could say that what contemporary "democracies" wish to impose upon the planet is an animal humanism. In it man only exists as worthy of pity. Man is a *pitiable animal*' (2007: 175). Using the word 'animal' to define a humanism that is problematically tied to the political model of neoliberal democracy, Badiou's discourse betrays a sense that animals are only worthy of pity. They represent a kind of melancholic passivity rather than an active political agency. For Badiou, animal humanism – 'the deep animality, to which man is *reduced* by contemporary humanism', the 'representation of man which *reduces* him to his animal body' – is to be rejected (176; 174; italics mine). With echoes of Kant's view, which opened this chapter, Badiou repeatedly describes how 'man' is 'reduced' to a seemingly lower state of animality which is the mere 'infrastructure' that he 'contains'. Regardless of the merits of Badiou's rigorous and urgent critique of neoliberal ideology, there is never any sense that the human *as* animal will lead the way to revolutionary politics. We might say his position is the inverse of posthumanism: both Badiou and the posthumanists declare that the human is an animal, but for Badiou this signals a retreat from real politics while for the posthumanists it marks its new condition. Posthumanism sees the animality of the human as the beginning of a radical political and philosophical debate, whereas for Badiou 'animal humanism wants to abolish the discussion itself' (177).

Posthumanism therefore offers both a challenge to the liberal humanist subject and exposes limitations in supposedly radical breaks from neoliberalism. Contrary to what Badiou and Žižek would argue, the concerns of posthumanism shouldn't be aligned with a 'postmodernist malaise' that dispenses with radical political agency. Indeed, more dialogue between posthumanist and neo-Marxist philosophy might create openings for a new political ontology that takes proper account of animals in their material relations. Posthumanism actually develops out of the same historical legacy of humanism and anti-humanism that Badiou delineates, and many posthumanist animal theorists share a sense that the 'political subject' needs to be recuperated after the relativism of postmodernism. In *The Posthuman*, Rosi Braidotti argues for a 'critical posthumanism' that will meet many of the political challenges raised above (2013: 51). Rather than dispensing with subjectivity Braidotti 'works instead towards elaborating alternative ways of conceptualizing the human subject' and aims to 'develop affirmative perspectives on the posthuman subject' (37; 45). Braidotti reminds us that posthumanism is fundamentally post-anthropocentric, but frames this post-anthropocentrism not as a turning away from subjectivity but as a way to experiment with and affirm new subjectivities: 'The key question for me is: what understandings of contemporary subjectivity and subject-formation are enabled by a post-anthropocentric approach?' (58) Thoroughly embodied and embedded in a lively material world, this view of subjectivity is open to the animality of the human as well as to other animals:

> The vitality of their bond is based on sharing this planet, territory or environment on terms that are no longer so clearly hierarchical, nor self-evident. This vital interconnection posits a qualitative shift of the relationship away from species-ism and towards . . . a new political frame . . . an affirmative project in response to the commodification of Life in all its forms, that is the opportunistic logic of advanced capitalism. (72)

Braidotti's subject is humble, anti-individualist, post-anthropocentric and yet wholeheartedly engaged in a political struggle that combines 'critique with creativity' (104). Like Braidotti, Wolfe opens up the possibility for nonhumans to be thought of as subjects in the posthuman landscape – his exposing of speciesism is precisely framed around the idea that it dictates who can be subjects, rather than necessarily wanting to dispense with the subject altogether. He wants to resist those who make 'even the *possibility* of subjectivity coterminous with the species barrier' – such a move is 'deeply problematic, if not clearly untenable' (Wolfe 2010: 1). There may remain contradictions and challenges in recuperating any kind of 'subject' – a term so thoroughly bound up with humanist discourses – for non-anthropocentric ends, but Braidotti's posthuman subject offers one alternative to supposedly more radical philosophers who often revert to anthropocentrism.

New Materialist Alliances and the Object of Politics

The definition of 'posthuman theory' as a 'vital materialism' that 'contests the arrogance of anthropocentrism and the "exceptionalism" of the Human as a transcendental category' (Braidotti 2013: 66) leads to affinities with another emerging critical field known as 'new materialism'. As with posthumanist theory, new materialism aims to move beyond the postmodernist emphasis on constructivism and critique of language and subjectivity. But the emphasis of new materialism is, like other growing theoretical modes of enquiry such as 'object oriented ontology' (Harman 2011) and 'speculative realism' (Mackay 2007a, 2007b), less on subjectivity and more on objectivity. As Diana Coole and Samantha Frost outline in their agenda-setting volume *New Materialisms*:

> over the past three decades or so theorists have radicalized the way
> they understand subjectivity, discovering its efficacy in constructing
> even the most apparently natural phenomena while insisting upon its
> embeddedness in dense networks of power that outrun its control and
> constitute its wilfulness. Yet it is on subjectivity that their gaze has
> focused . . . it is now time to subject objectivity and material reality to a
> similarly radical reappraisal. (2010: 2)

As is vibrantly evident throughout Coole and Frost's collection, the aim of new materialists is to broaden and deepen our exploration of materiality without falling into reductive and naively positivist explanations of the material world.

One of the central features of new materialism is a posthumanist, non-anthropocentric view of materiality where the agency of matter itself is recognised (rather than being seen as something to be captured and controlled by humans). In fact, this approach 'does not even privilege human bodies' because 'all bodies, including those of animals . . . evince certain capacities for agency. As a consequence, the human species, and the qualities of self-reflection, self-awareness, and rationality traditionally used to distinguish it from the rest of nature, may now', according to Coole and Frost, 'seem little more than contingent and provisional forms or processes within a broader evolutionary or cosmic productivity' (20). Put into perspective, humanity is no longer considered the crowning achievement of life on earth, nor as the only concern in socio-economic frameworks. By placing materiality, rather than a privileged 'human', at the centre of enquiry, our sense of human superiority is undermined and in its place a more complicated distribution of agencies emerges. Jane Bennett argues in *Vibrant Matter* that such agencies have political import: 'politics is itself often construed as an exclusively human domain' and so 'what registers on it is a set of material constraints on or a context for human action'. By broadening the scope of political agency and responsibility beyond anthropocentrism we locate the difference between 'vital materialism' and the historical materialism associated with Marxism (2010: xvi).

Although not explicitly concerned with animals, Karen Barad's *Meeting the Universe Halfway* explores this posthumanist materialism in her analysis of the philosophical implications of quantum physics and the effect of this on our understanding of agency. Barad's concept of 'agential realism', which draws on theorists such as Haraway, Foucault and Judith Butler, and is influenced by the quantum physicist Niels Bohr, offers a 'posthumanist performative' account of reality which takes account of the liveliness of matter. In this view 'agency is not an attribute' of a being or thing, subject or object, but is entangled in 'the ongoing reconfigurations of the world' (Barad 2007: 135; 141). Barad introduces the term 'intra-action', as distinct from 'interaction', to express this always already entangled state of agency:

> 'intra-action' *signifies the mutual constitution of entangled agencies.* That is, in contrast to the usual 'interaction,' which assumes that there are separate individual agencies that precede their interaction, the notion of intra-action recognizes that distinct agencies do not precede, but rather emerge through, their intra-action. It is important to note that the 'distinct' agencies are only distinct in a relational, not an absolute, sense . . . *agencies are only distinct in relation to their mutual entanglement; they don't exist as individual elements.* (33)

A consequence of 'intra-action' is that what we call 'human' *emerges* within a broader field of materiality; we can't distinguish human actors in advance, meaning that there is no *a priori* separation between human and nonhuman, culture and nature – this echoes Haraway, who notes the influence of 'intra-action' on her thought (2008: 17; 165; 285). Barad therefore presents a non-anthropocentric conception of agency: 'refusing the anthropocentrisms of humanism and antihumanism, *posthumanism* marks the practice of accounting for the boundary-making practices by which the "human" and its others are differentially delineated and defined' (2007: 136). New materialism shifts the discussion away from subject/object, human/nonhuman dichotomies and towards messier entanglements of agency.

Within contemporary theory, then, new materialists and animal theorists often share a non-anthropocentric – or to use Braidotti's term 'post-anthropocentric' – approach to matter and life. But rather than concluding that this marks a clear shift from one set of thinkers (postmodernists) to another (posthumanists), it also tells us something about those thinkers usually labelled 'poststructuralist' who are often too quickly conflated with postmodernist theorists and critics. Some of the roots of posthumanism are actually traceable to poststructuralist theory, which therefore calls for a re-evaluation of the diverse range of thinkers who are grouped under this latter term. The obvious example is Deleuze, who, as we saw above, is interested in non-anthropocentric (we might even say posthumanist) modes of material life. Deleuze's philosophy expresses a 'material vitalism' (Deleuze and Guattari

2004: 454) or what Elizabeth Grosz describes as 'a kind of supersaturated materialism . . . that incorporates that which is commonly opposed to it – the ideal, the conceptual, the mind, or consciousness' (2011: 43). The connections Deleuze makes between the vitality of life and matter have had a marked influence on Braidotti, as well as the new materialists more broadly, and many of the primary influences on Deleuze – the likes of Spinoza, Leibniz, Nietzsche and Bergson – are also central to these (re)emerging debates about materiality. It is worth noting, too, that in *Expressionism in Philosophy: Spinoza*, Deleuze himself used the phrase 'new "materialism"' to describe the conceptualisation of expressive materiality that became a prominent part of the anti-Cartesian reaction in the late seventeenth century (Deleuze 1992: 321). In a different way, contemporary new materialist theory is also indebted to Derrida. As will be seen in Chapters 3 and 4, Derrida's later writings very clearly place animals at the centre of his thought. And critics are now pointing out how, throughout his work as a whole, even though he may be more invested in exploring processes of representation and signification and in exposing linguistically framed views of the world, his project of deconstruction profoundly reconceptualises the relationship between language and materiality (Kirby 2011). Whether we are moving towards genuinely *new* materialisms, or revising earlier thought, there are in contemporary debates many ontological and political alliances to be forged with animal theory.

UNCOMFORTABLE ANALOGIES: *THE LIVES OF ANIMALS*

Reading animals literally makes us uncomfortable. This sentence can be read in two ways. Firstly, to read *animals* literally, as animals rather than stand-ins for something else, makes us uncomfortable because it feels naive or too straightforward. We think it means that we are not really thinking. Secondly, it literally makes *us* uncomfortable in the sense that such discomfort is seated in our bodies, in our very being. We are forced to confront uncomfortable truths about the way that our culture, our language and our thoughts have become distanced from animal being and from our own animality. In many ways the animal ontologies presented by Nietzsche, Deleuze and Guattari and Haraway suggest that reading animals literally could provide an opening onto a different mode of thought. For reading animals *as animals* raises questions about exactly what those animals, the ones we read about, or encounter in reality, or find in ourselves, really *are*. Reading and thinking about animal ontology makes the very concept of 'being' an uncomfortable one, one that cannot be easily attached to settled categories of culture or nature, humanity or animality.

J. M. Coetzee's 'lecture narrative' (1999: 73), *The Lives of Animals*, presents a bestiary of literary and philosophical animals and challenges us to read and think literally about them. What becomes clear as the protagonist, the fictional novelist Elizabeth Costello, gives her lecture to an audience at Appleton College, is the significance of those moments in the text which address not just the issue of making us feel uncomfortable about the way we mistreat animals in the contemporary world (including the issues around eating animals, to be addressed in Chapter 4), but which also unsettle our sense of being human as distinct from animal being. Costello describes, for example, how she has 'always been uncomfortable' with the Cartesian view of animals as machines (33). She takes aim at Kant's focus on reason because he 'does not pursue, with regard to animals, the implications of his intuition that reason may be not the being of the universe but on the contrary merely the being of the human brain' (23). As we saw at the opening of this chapter, Kant identifies reason as the capacity through which humanity is 'distinguished from animality' (Kant 1996: 154). Rather than creating a hierarchical divide based on thought and reason, Costello argues that human and animal being is about 'fullness, embodiedness, the sensation of being' (Coetzee 1999: 33). It is telling that such claims make her son, John, and his wife, Norma, shift their bodies uncomfortably in the audience: 'Norma, sitting beside him, gives a sigh of exasperation so slight that he alone hears it. But then, he alone was meant to hear it'; 'A little snort from Norma. He finds her hand, and squeezes it' (32).

As part of her challenge to fixed notions of a hierarchical divide between human and animal being, Costello draws two related analogies. The first occurs when she compares herself to Franz Kafka's ape from 'A Report to an Academy', his 1917 story about a primate who becomes human. The protagonist, Red Peter (the name given to him due to a gunshot wound on his left cheek when captured which left a 'naked, red scar'), recounts the story of attempts to bring his 'ape nature' 'under control' (Kafka 2005: 251). Recalling her last talk at Appleton College two years previously, Costello tells her audience, and her readers: 'On that occasion I felt a little like Red Peter myself and I said so. Today the feeling is even stronger, for reasons that I hope will become clearer to you.' But, she stresses, this analogy is not merely a self-deprecating quip:

'The comparison I have just drawn between myself and Kafka's ape might be taken as such a lighthearted remark, meant to set you at ease, meant to say I am just an ordinary person, neither a god nor a beast. Even those among you who read Kafka's story of the ape who performs before human beings as an allegory of Kafka the Jew performing for Gentiles may nevertheless – in view of the fact that I am not a Jew – have done me the kindness of taking the comparison at face value, that is to say, ironically.

'I want to say at the outset that that was not how my remark – the remark that I feel like Red Peter – was intended. I did not intend it ironically. It means what it says. I say what I mean. I am an old woman. I do not have the time any longer to say things I do not mean.' (Coetzee 1999: 18)

In turning to the ape in Kafka's story, Costello runs the risk of reading this literary animal too literally: 'like most writers, I have a literal cast of mind ... When Kafka writes about an ape, I take him to be talking in the first place about an ape' (32). In Costello's view, the ape demands attention before we consider metaphorical, symbolic, or allegorical meanings – a theme she develops later when speaking to students about how to read Ted Hughes' animal poems (50–3). This also echoes a comment Coetzee himself made in an interview when bemoaning the fact that reviewers of his books, most notably *Disgrace*, often ignore or only incidentally register the presence of animals: 'In this respect they – naturally – mirror the way in which animals are treated in the world we live in, namely as unimportant existences of which we need take notice only when their lives cross ours' (quoted in Dawn and Singer 2010: 110). In drawing an analogy between herself and the ape, Costello wants to confront her audience with the uncomfortable reality of human ignorance about animal being.

Costello speaks of an ontological wound that is bound to a human being who excises her or his own animality. She asserts that 'Red Peter was not an investigator of primate behaviour', but an embodied, wounded being: Red Peter is 'a branded, marked, wounded animal presenting himself as speaking testimony to a gathering of scholars'. She herself is also 'an animal exhibiting, yet not exhibiting, to a gathering of scholars, a wound, which I cover up under my clothes but touch on in every word I speak' (Coetzee 1999: 26). Underneath Costello's clothes her animality is trying to express itself; these wounded animal bodies include her own. As Cora Diamond has argued, 'the life of this speaking and wounded and clothed animal is one of the "lives of animals" that the story is about' (2008: 47). The shared, exposed materiality of bodies, whether human or nonhuman, are presented to the audience and to the reader, and this poses a challenge to those who begin sentences about animals with the words 'they have no consciousness *therefore*'. Costello interrogates the assumptions behind this phrasing: 'Therefore what? Therefore we are free to use them for our own ends? Therefore we are free to kill them? Why? What is so special about the form of consciousness we recognize that makes killing a bearer of it a crime while killing an animal goes unpunished?' (Coetzee 1999: 44). These are uncomfortable ethical questions about our exploitation of fellow beings that can only be addressed by challenging the all-too-comfortable conceptualisation of the divide between human and animal being.

While this first analogy works towards a shared ontology of humans and animals, Costello undermines it by making a more uncomfortable comparison that rests on those ontological assumptions she seemingly wants to challenge. This becomes clear when, in arguing about the way animals are treated by humans, she draws an analogy between the industrial slaughter of animals and the holocaust:

> '"They went like sheep to the slaughter." "They died like animals."
> "The Nazi butchers killed them." Denunciation of the camps
> reverberates so fully with the language of the stockyard and
> slaughterhouse that it is barely necessary for me to prepare the ground
> for the comparison I am about to make. The crime of the Third Reich,
> says the voice of accusation, was to treat people like animals.' (20)

In making this statement the problem is precisely that Costello fails to prepare the ontological 'ground' for it. Whereas above she drew an analogy between human and animal in order to unsettle categories of being, here her comparison too neatly equates two very different events. To decry the treatment of people *like* animals is to imply, however inadvertently, that there are two essential ontological categories of 'human' and 'animal' and that animality is the lower form of life. When Costello goes on to claim that the killing of animals today 'rivals' (a curiously competitive term to use in this context) that of the holocaust we have to ask how this moral judgement tallies with the ontological assumptions her argument has so far put forward. Moreover, for all her critique of Descartes and Kant, Costello ironically turns to the seemingly boundless human capacity for thought as a reason why we should have no excuses for failing to sympathise with cruelty towards nonhuman beings: 'there is no limit to the extent to which we can think ourselves into the being of another. There are no bounds to the sympathetic imagination' (35) – in this she responds to Nagel's argument in 'What is it Like to be a Bat?', discussed in Chapter 1. Intended by Costello as an ethical call, the problem with this second analogy is that it departs from the more complicated and uncomfortable ontological relation that her first analogy implied.

For Donna Haraway, Costello's moral argument is problematic because it overshadows any effort to discuss real animal beings. It is an example of how for Costello 'actually existing animals do not seem to be present'; they are lost amidst 'a radical language of animal rights' that makes 'universal claims' (Haraway 2008: 81). For Haraway, the equating of the holocaust and industrial factory farming abstracts the lives of animals from the debate. It is seen as a sweeping, dogmatic statement which pays little attention to the specificity of animal and human being: 'She practices the enlightenment method of comparative history in order to fix the awful equality of slaughter. Meat eating is like the Holocaust; meat eating is the Holocaust' (81). Too comfortable in its logic,

Costello's analogy also receives a riposte later in *The Lives of Animals* from the poet Abraham Stern, who fails to show for the follow-up session to the lecture the next day. He instead leaves a note explaining:

> You took over for your own purposes the familiar comparison between the murdered Jew of Europe and slaughtered cattle. The Jews died like cattle, therefore cattle die like Jews, you say. That is a trick with words which I will not accept. You misunderstand the nature of likenesses; I would even say you misunderstand wilfully, to the point of blasphemy. Man is made in the likeness of God but God does not have the likeness of man. If Jews were treated like cattle, it does not follow that cattle are treated like Jews. The inversion insults the memory of the dead. It trades on the horrors of the camps in a cheap way. (Coetzee 1999: 49)

Stern shares with Haraway a sense that the comparison between the slaughter of animals and the holocaust is misjudged. But Stern's argument is not without its own problems. He correctly states that these two events are not equivalent, but note how he allows the first part of the comparison – 'Jews died like cattle' – to pass unremarked. In the same way that the second part of the analogy – 'cattle die like Jews' – is flawed because it assumes knowledge of the Jews who died in the holocaust and equates this with a qualitatively different kind of suffering, so the first part is problematic because it assumes knowledge of the experiences of cattle and equates it with a qualitatively different kind of suffering. Stern's willingness to accept the premise that 'Jews died like cattle' but reject the logic of the reverse claim suggests that he is, perhaps, too comfortable with the use of the slaughter of meat as a figure of speech and blind to the ways in which this also trades on suffering.

The Lives of Animals therefore exposes the limitations of analogy in attempts to express animal ontology. A problem is created by the very dynamic of trying to address ontological questions with the method of analogy, which presupposes that there are two entities or events which we know and which we can then equate. While in the first analogy Costello presents an uncomfortable relation between human and animal, in the second she presents all-too-comfortable simplification. If it is a challenge for readers to read animals literally, the challenge for writers – whether of literature or theory – is to find modes of expression that manage to break free of familiar categories and relations. This might explain why Coetzee chooses a hybrid narrative form which itself unsettles generic conventions: Coetzee 'is doing philosophy and literature through the writing of fiction' and 'is as much thinking about the value of philosophy, or of literature, as he is probing our disvaluation of animals' (Flynn 2010: 318). Whether in literary philosophy or philosophical literature, the value in challenging hierarchical divides between humans and animals is undermined if in its place they settle too neatly into analogies that erase asymmetrical histories and experiences. The real challenge for animal ontology is to transform the relation between human and animal, and their shared 'fullness of being' (33), into one of creative discomfort.

KEY TEXTS

Badiou, Alain (2007), 'The Joint Disappearances of Man and God', in *The Century*, trans. Alberto Toscano, Cambridge: Polity.
Braidotti, Rosi (2013), *The Posthuman*, Cambridge: Polity.
Coetzee, J. M. (1999), *The Lives of Animals*, ed. Amy Gutmann, Princeton: Princeton University Press.
Coole, Diana and Samantha Frost (eds) (2010), *New Materialisms: Ontology, Agency, and Politics*, Durham NC: Duke University Press.
Deleuze, Gilles and Félix Guattari (1986), *Kafka: Toward a Minor Literature*, trans. Dana Polan, Minneapolis: University of Minnesota Press.
Deleuze, Gilles and Félix Guattari (2004), *A Thousand Plateaus: Capitalism and Schizophrenia*, trans. Brian Massumi, London: Continuum.
Haraway, Donna (2003), *The Companion Species Manifesto: Dogs, People, and Significant Otherness*, Chicago: Prickly Paradigm Press.
Haraway, Donna (2008), *When Species Meet*, Minneapolis: University of Minnesota Press.
Kafka, Franz (2005), 'A Report to An Academy', in Nahum N. Glatzer (ed.), *Franz Kafka: The Complete Short Stories*, London: Vintage, pp. 250–62.
Nietzsche, Friedrich (2003a), *Thus Spoke Zarathustra*, trans. R. J. Hollingdale, London: Penguin.
Wolfe, Cary (2010), *What is Posthumanism?*, Minneapolis: University of Minnesota Press.

FURTHER READING

Acampora, Christa Davis and Ralph R. Acampora (eds) (2004), *A Nietzschean Bestiary: Becoming Animal Beyond Docile and Brutal*, Lanham: Rowman & Littlefield.
Adorno, Theodor W. and Max Horkheimer (1997), *Dialectic of Enlightenment*, trans. John Cumming, London: Verso.
Ansell-Pearson, Keith (1999), 'Bergson and Creative Evolution/Involution', in John Mullarkey (ed.), *The New Bergson*, Manchester: Manchester University Press, pp. 146–67.

Badiou, Alain (2005), 'Truths and Justice', in *Metapolitics*, trans. Jason Barker, London: Verso, pp. 96–106.

Badiou, Alain (2010), 'The Idea of Communism', in *The Communist Hypothesis*, trans. David Macey and Steve Corcoran, London: Verso, pp. 229–60.

Badiou, Alain and Slavoj Žižek (2009), *Philosophy in the Present*, trans. Peter Thomas and Alberto Toscano, Cambridge: Polity.

Baker, Steve (2002), 'What Does Becoming-Animal Look Like?', in Nigel Rothfels (ed.), *Representing Animals*, Bloomington: Indiana University Press, pp. 67–98.

Barad, Karen (2007), *Meeting the Universe Halfway: Quantum Physics and the Entanglement of Matter and Meaning*, Durham NC: Duke University Press.

Bennett, Jane (2010), *Vibrant Matter: A Political Ecology of Things*, Durham NC: Duke University Press.

Bergson, Henri (1998), *Creative Evolution*, trans. Arthur Mitchell, New York: Dover.

Braidotti, Rosi (2006), 'Posthuman, All Too Human: Towards a New Process Ontology', *Theory Culture Society* 23, 197–208.

Brown, Lori (2007), 'Becoming-Animal in the Flesh: Expanding the Ethical Reach of Deleuze and Guattari's Tenth Plateau', *PhaenEx* 2.2, 260–78.

Calarco, Matthew (2008), *Zoographies: The Question of the Animal from Heidegger to Derrida*, New York: Columbia University Press.

Danta, Chris and Dimitris Vardoulakis (eds) (2008), 'Special Issue: The Political Animal', *SubStance* 37.3.

Dawn, Karen and Peter Singer (2010), 'Converging Conviction: Coetzee and His Characters on Animals', in Anton Leist and Peter Singer (eds), *J. M. Coetzee and Ethics: Philosophical Perspectives on Literature*, New York: Columbia University Press, pp. 109–18.

Deleuze, Gilles (1991), *Bergsonism*, trans. Hugh Tomlinson and Barbara Habberjam, New York: Zone Books.

Deleuze, Gilles (1992), *Expressionism in Philosophy: Spinoza*, trans. Martin Joughin, New York: Zone Books.

Deleuze, Gilles (2005), *Francis Bacon: The Logic of Sensation*, trans. Daniel W. Smith, London: Continuum.

Deleuze, Gilles (2006), *Nietzsche and Philosophy*, trans. Hugh Tomlinson, London: Continuum.

Deleuze, Gilles and Claire Parnet (2012), *From A to Z*, dir. Pierre-André Boutang, trans. Charles J. Stivale, Los Angeles: Semiotext(e), DVD.

Derrida, Jacques (2009), *The Beast and the Sovereign*, vol. 1, trans. Geoffrey Bennington, Chicago: University of Chicago Press.

Diamond, Cora (2008), 'The Difficulty of Reality and the Difficulty of Philosophy', in Stanley Cavell et al., *Philosophy and Animal Life*, New York: Columbia University Press, pp. 43–90.

Dolphijn, Rick and Iris van der Tuin (eds) (2012), *New Materialism: Interviews and Cartographies*, Open Humanities Press.

Flynn, Jennifer (2010), 'The Lives of Animals and the Form-Content Connection', in Anton Leist and Peter Singer (eds), *J.M. Coetzee and Ethics: Philosophical Perspectives on Literature*, New York: Columbia University Press, pp. 317–36.

Groff, Peter S. (2004), 'Who is Zarathustra's Ape?', in Christa Davis Acampora and Ralph R. Acampora (eds), *A Nietzschean Bestiary: Becoming Animal Beyond Docile and Brutal*, Lanham: Rowman & Littlefield, pp. 17–31.

Grosz, Elizabeth (2011), *Becoming Undone: Darwinian Reflections on Life, Politics, and Art*, Durham NC: Duke University Press.

Harman, Graham (2011), *The Quadruple Object*, Alresford: Zero Books.

Haraway, Donna (1989), *Primate Visions: Gender, Race, and Nature in the World of Modern Science*, New York: Routledge.

Haraway, Donna (1991), *Simians, Cyborgs, and Women: The Reinvention of Nature*, New York: Routledge.

Hatab, Lawrence (2005), *Nietzsche's Life Sentences: Coming to Terms with Eternal Recurrence*, New York: Routledge.

Hayles, N. Katherine (1999), *How We Became Posthuman: Virtual Bodies in Cybernetics, Literature, and Informatics*, Chicago: University of Chicago Press.

Kant, Immanuel (1996), *The Metaphysics of Morals*, Cambridge: Cambridge University Press.

Kirby, Vicki (2011), 'Anthropology Diffracted: Originary Humanicity', in *Quantum Anthropologies: Life at Large*, Durham NC: Duke University Press.

Langer, Monika (1999), 'The Role and Status of Animals in Nietzsche's Philosophy', in H. Peter Steeves (ed.), *Animal Others: On Ethics, Ontology, and Animal Life*, Albany: State University of New York Press, pp. 75–92.

Latour, Bruno (1993), *We Have Never Been Modern*, trans. Catherine Porter, Cambridge MA: Harvard University Press.

Lawlor, Leonard (2008), 'Following the Rats: Becoming-Animal in Deleuze and Guattari', *SubStance* 37.3, 169–87.

Lemm, Vanessa (2009), *Nietzsche's Animal Philosophy: Culture, Politics, and the Animality of the Human Being*, New York: Fordham University Press.

Mackay, Robin (ed.) (2007a), 'Speculative Realism', *Collapse: Philosophical Research and Development* 2, Falmouth: Urbanomic.

Mackay, Robin (ed.) (2007b), 'Unknown Deleuze (+Speculative Realism)', *Collapse: Philosophical Research and Development* 3, Falmouth: Urbanomic.

More, Max and Natasha Vita-More (eds) (2013), *The Transhumanist Reader*, Oxford: Wiley-Blackwell.

Nietzsche, Friedrich (1982), *Daybreak: Thoughts on the Prejudices of Morality*, trans. R. J. Hollingdale, Cambridge: Cambridge University Press.

Nietzsche, Friedrich (1994), *Human, All Too Human*, trans. Marion Faber and Stephen Lehmann, London: Penguin.

Nietzsche, Friedrich (1998), *On the Genealogy of Morals*, trans. Douglas Smith, Oxford: Oxford University Press.

Nietzsche, Friedrich (2003b), *Twilight of the Idols* and *The Anti-Christ*, trans. R. J. Hollingdale, London: Penguin.

Nietzsche, Friedrich (2006), *The Gay Science*, trans. Thomas Common, Mineola: Dover.

Nietzsche, Friedrich (2007), 'Homer's Contest', in *On the Genealogy of Morality and Other Writings*, trans. Carol Diethe, Cambridge: Cambridge University Press, pp. 174–82.

Sanbonmatsu, John (ed.) (2011), *Critical Theory and Animal Liberation* (2011), Maryland: Rowman & Littlefield.

Traisnel, Antoine (2012), 'Zarathustra's Philosafari', *Humanimalia* 3.2, 83–106.

Turner, Lynn (2010). 'When Species Kiss: Some Recent Correspondence Between Animots', *Humanimalia* 2:1, 60–85.

Wolfe, Cary (ed) (2003a), *Zoontologies: The Question of the Animal*, Minneapolis: University of Minnesota Press.

Wolfe, Cary (2003b), *Animal Rites: American Culture, the Discourse of Species, and Posthumanist Theory*, Chicago: University of Chicago Press.

Slavoj Žižek (2008), 'Fear Thy Neighbour As Thyself!', in *Violence*, London: Profile Books, pp. 34–62.

CHAPTER 3

Animal Life

EVERYDAY ANIMALS

The majority of human interactions with animals involve a relatively small variety of species in everyday environments. When we think of the animals we most frequently encounter, it is usually those that are part of agricultural or familial domestication: either livestock, that is the sheep, cattle and pigs all thought to have first been domesticated between 7,000 and 11,000 years ago; or the animals now commonly kept as pets including cats, first domesticated 8,500 years ago, and dogs, first domesticated from anywhere between 30,000 and over 100,000 years ago (DeMello 2012: 85–6). The lives of such animals have, then, a long history in which they have been tamed to benefit humans in some way. Today, the human use of certain species is so extensive that it is almost impossible to imagine passing twenty-four hours without coming into contact with domesticated animals or animal products. To take just one example, we encounter cows on a daily basis in some form. Most obviously, cattle are made into meat and milk products, where just over half of a slaughtered cow is turned into beef products to be eaten. But there are far more uses for the dead cow, which is added to everyday items that we don't always think of as having bovine origins: the carcass, which includes the bones, hide, fat and organs, is 'broken down by renderers into a range of other substances. For example, beef fat and fatty acids are used in shoe creams, crayons, floor wax, margarine, cosmetics, deodorants, detergents, soaps, perfumes, insecticides, linoleum, insulation and refrigerants' (Velten 2007: 157–8). The term 'livestock' seems an odd choice to categorise animals that become an everyday part of human life precisely as a result of their death.

In the case of cats, dogs and other animals found in our homes, the reasons for domestication, and the way humans *use* animals, is less obvious. On the one hand we don't expect much from our pets other than to be our companions, but on the other hand their function has in some ways been to replace the growing absence of other domesticated animals from everyday life. While animals have been kept in domestic spaces since antiquity, the modern form of pet ownership – where the domestic animal provides companionship – interacts in an important way with a change in the domestication of livestock animals used for food and work: 'widespread ownership of animals with, as the legal definition would have it, no utilitarian function, emerges as a category during the sixteenth century, a time when domestic livestock – cows, pigs, were being removed from the home'. Therefore, at the same time as 'one animal – the domestic (and therefore edible) – is removed from close contact with humans, so, another – individualized (and therefore inedible) – enters' (Fudge 2002: 28). Today, pet ownership has become commonplace, with numbers growing exponentially in the last 100 years. The *Pet Food Manufacturers Association* estimates that as of 2013 there were 8.5 million cats and 8.5 million dogs kept as pets in the UK, while the *American Veterinary Medical Association*'s 2012 survey calculated just under 70 and 75 million pet dogs and cats respectively. Just as industrial agriculture has become a huge part of today's global economy, so too have pets become big business, where billions are spent every year on the pets themselves as well as on food, toys and even clothing (DeMello 2011: 80).

Livestock animals, and in particular the complex and charged ethical debates around how they are used and abused by humans, will be explored in more detail in Chapter 4, but the current chapter considers the relationship between humans and their pets. We have already seen how pets play an important role in theorising animals, whether we consider Lacan's boxer, Justine (see Chapter 1), or Haraway's Australian Shepherd, Cayenne (see Chapter 2 and below). It is hardly surprising that dogs and, as we will see, cats, should occupy an important position for animal theorists, because in many ways pets are a privileged kind of domesticated animal in western cultures: they are afforded a great amount of time and care; we would never think about eating them; we react with shock and unease if we see harm being done to them; and they are a fundamental part of the formation of the family. Pets seem to mean *more* to most humans than other animals. Yet they can also be thought of as *less*-than-animal precisely because of this: their breeding is often carefully controlled by humans; they cannot take care of themselves if left alone for long periods; they are, perhaps, more associated with culture than nature. These are some of the paradoxical issues theorists of human-pet relations have been most keen to explore.

Pets

Some critics have been scathing in their view of human dominance over subservient pets. Gary Francione provides a clear example of this, arguing against the widespread practice whereby 'pets are our property': 'Dogs, cats, hamsters, rabbits, and other animals are mass produced like bolts in a factory or, in the case of birds and exotic animals, are captured in the wild and transported long distances, during which journey many of them die' (2000: 169). Francione draws attention here to the ways in which pets are part of global networks of capitalism. Turned into commodities, the relationship between human and pet becomes one of ownership and control, where pets are dependent on humans for almost every aspect of their life, resulting in a thoroughly unequal power dynamic. As a result Francione adopts the view that while those domestic animals currently alive should be looked after well (and it is worth remembering that sometimes pets are cruelly treated or neglected), 'we should not continue to bring more animals into existence so that we may own them as pets' (170). Some have even focused on this issue of ownership and control to draw analogies with human slavery: in *The Dreaded Comparison* Marjorie Spiegel argues that 'the relationship between a dog and his master' is an example of a 'slave/slave-owner relationship'. Dog owners, in this argument, value displays of obedience and punish behaviours that don't conform to their wishes: 'All independent actions are thus discouraged, and the dog learns that he will win approval – and avoid future beatings and punishments – by suppressing his own desires' (Spiegel 1996: 41). Dogs are often ranked based on the qualities and behaviours of their breed, with purebreds highly sought after. Even if we don't want to concur wholly with Spiegel's point, which doesn't quite do justice to the complex asymmetries involved in the treatment of animals and slaves, there does exist a problematic relation between the desire for purebreds, the value placed on them, and racist discourses of purity. Such critiques take aim at a global scale of control, exposing how pet ownership might intersect, whether deliberately or inadvertently, with other disturbing power dynamics.

When we think about pet ownership on a more personal level, in its everyday realities, the above critiques appear to be overstated. We might wonder, for example, how a pet that adds so richly to family life could be understood as a victim of cruelty. And yet, some have critiqued pet ownership precisely as a result of its integration into modern family dynamics. John Berger argues in 'Why Look at Animals?' that pet ownership is indicative of a 'universal but personal withdrawal into the private small family unit, decorated or furnished with mementoes from the outside world, which is such a distinguishing feature of consumer societies'. For the pet this means confinement within a domestic arena where it is 'either sterilized or sexually isolated, extremely limited in its exercise, deprived of almost all other animal contact, and fed with artificial foods'. Pets are not allowed to be animals, then, and instead become 'creatures of their owner's way of life' (Berger 2009: 24–5). We make animals dependent on us because we depend so much on *them* for emotional consolation. This view proposes that the relationship between owner and pet is both anthropomorphic and anthropocentric. And as James Serpell shows in his essay 'People in Disguise', a dark reality awaits many pet animals who display non-anthropomorphic behaviour: 'Whenever there is a mismatch or incompatibility between an animal's behaviour and its owner's anthropomorphic expectations, the animal risks either being punished and abused for its perceived "misbehaviour" or being disposed of' (2005: 131). The implication of such critiques is that owning pets may make us more compassionate towards (some) domestic animals, but doesn't necessarily do anything to make us care more about other animals and may even distract us from these deeper structural problems that lead to their exploitation.

To present a purely cynical view of human-pet relations would, however, be to ignore the very important everyday encounters with pets that prompt humans to think about nonhuman life. Pets have not always existed, and certainly not in the numbers and way that they do now – they are not, then, a *natural* feature of life – but in focusing solely on the problems betrayed by pet ownership we miss the importance of our encounters with these animals. Erica Fudge suggests that pets 'offer philosophers new ways of thinking'; the pet is 'not just the object of thought here, it is also the producer' (2008: 9). Seeing the pet as a producer, or subject, of thought means that we would have to consider not only the larger structural ways in which power dynamics play out, but also the ways in which pets can help us to reconceptualise how we think of the boundary between humanity and animality. Responding directly to Berger, Fudge takes offence at what she sees as his 'belittling of the pet': 'His argument that pets are somehow not fully animal (they are too humanized) implicitly proposes a category of the authentic animal' (24). In other words, there is a danger in Berger presenting animals as though they are only real, only truly *animal*, if they are inextricably tied to nature and excluded from human environments. Any animal, the argument goes, that depends on human cultural practices for its well-being does not truly have an animal identity. Moreover, in Berger's statement that pets are 'deprived of almost all other animal contact', Fudge finds the humanist assumption that humans are somehow separated from the animal kingdom and are not themselves animals. Berger misses the point that 'pets do have contact with one other animal in particular: the species Homo sapiens is central to all of their lives' (24).

Fudge is right to point to assumptions about the purity of categories implied by Berger's analysis, but the word 'central' in her own response betrays the fact that some level of anthropocentrism is implicit in the relationship between humans and pets. It is very important to remain open to the ways in which encounters with pet animals can transform our thoughts about human dominance, but at the same time we must remember that the way in which humans and animals enter into those encounters is asymmetrical. That pets spend time with another animal species in Homo sapiens cannot be denied, but this doesn't mean it is insignificant that those pets remain largely under the control of this one species. An issue remains as to how limited the experiences of pets are – including their experience with other animals, either of their own or different species – by being mainly contained within a human familial sphere. The real challenge is to critique this human centrality while not judging it to be necessarily indicative of the exploitation of domestic animals. It is in attempts to account for the differences between humans and pets, while at the same time considering how their shared spaces and experiences might be part of a less hierarchical relationship, that some of the most fascinating theoretical encounters with animals are located.

The animal that therefore I am

Nude Encounters and Little Cats

In *The Animal That Therefore I Am*, which collects material first presented at a conference in 1997, Jacques Derrida's encounter with his cat finds him in his bathroom 'caught naked, in silence, by the gaze of an animal' (2008: 3). The 'embarrassment' this event causes leads to a wide-ranging treatise on the relationship between humanity and animality (4). The first issue raised by Derrida is about the very experience of nudity which has been denied in animals:

> It is generally thought . . . that the property unique to animals, what
> in the last instance distinguishes them from man, is their being naked
> without knowing it. Not being naked therefore . . . They wouldn't be
> naked because they are naked. In principle, with the exception of man,
> no animal has ever thought to dress itself. Clothing would be proper to
> man, one of the "properties" of man . . . The animal, therefore, is not
> naked because it is naked. It doesn't feel its own nudity. There is no
> nudity "in nature". (5)

The terms 'naked' and 'nudity' are revealed as cultural constructions; they are products of human language and describe a phenomenon of the human body. Only humans cover up their bodies and therefore also their sex; only humans have to name an experience of 'shame'. The cat is 'naked without consciousness of being naked', whereas Derrida, clothed in consciousness, language and garments, finds himself not just ashamed but 'ashamed of being ashamed' (4–5).

The Animal That Therefore I Am does not, however, aim to express one clear divide between all humans (in culture) and cats (in nature). To begin with, Derrida stresses that he doesn't want his cat to be understood as a symbolic stand-in for all felines: 'the cat I am talking about is a real cat, truly, believe me, a little cat. It isn't', he adds, 'the *figure* of a cat. It doesn't silently enter the bedroom as an allegory for all the cats on the earth, the felines that traverse our myths and religions, literature and fables' (6). Derrida appears, then, to strip his cat of symbolism in an attempt to talk about 'the animal in itself' (3), the animal in its 'unsubstitutable singularity'. But in the process of insisting that his cat isn't a symbolic 'ambassador' for all cats (9), Derrida does point to a range of other felines, from the fables of La Fontaine to Lewis Carroll's *Alice in Wonderland*. In doing so, he self-reflexively acknowledges the difficulty in trying to talk about this 'real cat' in itself. As part of the wider signifying system through which humans think about animals, the meaning of this 'cat' that he writes about – as his earlier work on 'différance' would suggest – is bound up in 'infinite implication, the indefinite referral of signifier to signifier' (Derrida 2011: 29). From the bathroom to the page, Derridean deconstruction tells us that this 'cat' is a 'signifier' (sound-image) that cannot be neatly attached to a 'signified' (concept) let alone a 'referent' (material object) in the world. Indeed it is in challenging the authority of words that deconstruction itself has been described as revealing the 'animal-like' movements of both writing and reading (Wood 2014: 20; 66; 78; 2013: 26). Derrida's 'cat' doesn't settle into a generalisable figure that stands-in for all other felines, but nor does it stand alone as an individualised, real-life creature who is straightforwardly represented in language. This feline instead enters a textual and conceptual deconstruction of the human/animal binary that works through 'multiplying', 'complicating' and 'thickening' the line between humanity and animality (Derrida 2008: 29).

In following his cat, Derrida offers an example of how domestic animals might lead to philosophical thought: 'The animal looks at us, and we are naked before it. Thinking perhaps begins there' (29). He goes on to posit multiple questions which open up our conceptualisations of animal life more broadly:

> 'Does the animal think?' 'Does the animal produce representations?' a self, imagination, a relation to the future as such? Does the animal have not only signs but a language, and what language? Does the animal die? Does it laugh? Does it cry? Does it grieve? Does it get bored? Does it lie? Does it forgive? Does it sing? Does it invent? Does it invent music? Does it play music? Does it play? Does it offer hospitality? Does it offer? Does it give? Does it have hands? eyes? etc.? modesty? clothes? and the mirror? All these questions, and a large number of others that depend on them, are questions concerning what is proper to the animal. They are immense in terms of their history, their presuppositions, the complexity of their stakes. (63)

I know nothing about you and you know nothing about me makes anything infinitely possible between us

What is proper to animals is no longer decided, but is uncertain and therefore full of potential. Note that among these 'immense' questions Derrida raises the possibility that animals may have some experience of nudity: although in philosophy it is 'never asked', he poses 'the question of whether an animal can see *me* naked, and especially whether it can see *itself* naked' (59). Opening up questions about animals and animality necessitates a willingness to shift perspective from human views of animals onto the animals' views of humans and of themselves.

In raising these questions, Derrida seeks to undermine human-centred perspectives and superiority in a similar way to the sixteenth-century philosopher Michel de Montaigne. In his 'Apology for Raymond Sebond' Montaigne writes that it is due to 'vanity' that man

> separates himself from the horde of other creatures, carves out their
> shares to his fellows and companions the animals, and distributes
> among them such portions of faculties and powers as he sees fit. How
> does he know, by the force of his intelligence, the secret internal
> stirrings of animals? By what comparison between them and us does he
> infer the stupidity that he attributes to them?
>
> When I play with my cat, who knows if I am not a pastime to her
> more than she is to me? (1958: 331)

Bearing a striking resemblance to *The Animal That Therefore I Am* (despite Derrida's insistence that his little cat 'isn't Montaigne's cat' [2008: 6]), Montaigne moves from an encounter with his feline to a wider consideration of the capacities animals might have. He goes on to speculate as to: the 'reason and foresight' of honeybees and swallows (332–3); the 'full and complete communication' among cows, dogs and horses (331–2) and that such communication is a form of 'speech' (335); the 'reasoning' of a fox (337); the 'science and wisdom' in how goats, tortoises and elephants avoid or treat pain (339); and the 'intelligence' of dogs who help to guide men (340). Animals, he argues, 'do still other things which are far beyond our capacity, which we are so far from being able to imitate that we cannot even imagine them' (344). Where it might appear as though Montaigne strays into anthropomorphism, such a charge depends upon the anthropocentric belief, outlined in Chapter 1, that capacities like 'communication', 'reasoning' and 'intelligence' are solely reserved for the human. Montaigne concludes that 'it is not by a true judgement, but by foolish pride and stubbornness, that we set ourselves before the other animals and sequester ourselves from their condition and society' (358). If we seriously recognise animal capacities, we will realise 'that there is more difference between a given man and a given man than between a given animal and a given man' (342). It is easy to see why Derrida regards 'Apology for Raymond

Sebond' as 'one of the greatest pre- or anti-Cartesian texts on the animal that exists' (2008: 6).

Derrida follows Montaigne in being one of few philosophers to suggest that animals have 'a capacity to respond' (163). For too long philosophers have viewed humans as having the ability, through language, to 'respond', whereas animals merely 'react' in a pre-set manner to phenomena – this is an opposition that goes to the very heart of the Cartesian view of humans as thinking beings, and other animals as automata. Derrida recasts the debate about response so that it is no longer based on the view of animals lacking a human language; instead, he argues that we need to resist pre-determined and simplified oppositions between reaction and response. He expands on this point in *The Beast and the Sovereign*:

> By problematizing . . . the purity and indivisibility of a line between reaction and response, and especially the possibility of tracing this line between mankind *in general* and the animal *in general*, one runs the risk, as people notice and won't fail to complain to me about, of throwing doubt on all responsibility, all ethics, all decision. (2009: 119)

Here Derrida is drawing attention to a criticism often levelled when one begins to deconstruct the opposition between response and reaction: namely, that questions of responsibility and ethical accountability towards other humans are undermined by becoming relative. For Derrida, however, this openness to what response and responsibility means is precisely what is needed in ethics:

> having doubts about responsibility, decision, one's own being-ethical, can be, or so it seems to me, and ought perhaps to remain, the indefeasible essence of ethics, of decision, and of responsibility. Any knowledge, certainty, and firm theoretical assurance on this subject would suffice to confirm, precisely, the very thing that one is trying to deny, namely a reactionality in the response. (119–20)

When human responses become pre-set, they become merely reactions. Engaging questions of response and responsibility beyond the human realm allows us to welcome a whole range of animals into the kind of ethical considerations detailed in Chapter 4, but also displays an openness to those questions of animal capacities and experience listed above.

Derrida's work on animality attempts to complicate the homogeneous categorisation of 'the animal' set up, in singular opposition, against 'the human'. What we refer to as 'the animal' reduces a heterogeneous group of creatures to one homogeneous category. He therefore offers a neologism, 'animot', to capture the limitations of this reduction of the animal to a single homogenised category that is only concerned with reaction. When spoken, 'animot' is a homonym of the French plural 'animaux'. When written, it draws attention to the fact this is just a word – or 'mot' in French. Derrida details the following three elements of this word animot; firstly, 'to have the plural *animals* heard in the singular'; secondly, to 'bring us back to the word', to the fact that 'the voice that names and that names the thing as such' is precisely the human voice that deprives the animal of the word, of language, of response; and thirdly, to open up the possibility of seeing the lack of human speech as not being a lack at all 'but perhaps of acceding to a thinking . . . that thinks the absence of the name and of the word otherwise, and as something other than a privation' (2008: 48). While humans speak about animals using their own language, it would be arrogant to assume that the animals that do not access this same language are necessarily deprived. Again, Derrida echoes Montaigne, who wonders whether this 'defect that hinders communication between them and us' might not be 'just as much ours as theirs' (1958: 331). Rather than ascribing lack, we would do better to think of the ways in which animals form their own meaningful modes of communication.

Among the issues Derrida raises, he reminds us that encounters between human and animal are also 'on the threshold of sexual differences', therefore challenging the neat way human sexual difference is divided, which rarely takes account of the 'immense confusion' of sexual differences across a wide array of species (2008: 36; 59). While this aspect of Derrida's work is sometimes left unremarked by animal studies scholars, the related limits of animal difference and sexual difference are evident throughout the 'horde of animals' – from ants to monkeys, hedgehogs to horses – that appear in his writings long before his more explicit theorising of animality in *The Animal That Therefore I Am* (37). Amidst his discussion of his cat, Derrida points to one of his 'zootobiographical origins' described in 'A Silkworm of One's Own', an essay which ends with his childhood memory of looking after a box of silkworms which were 'beyond any sexual difference or rather any duality of the sexes, and even beyond any coupling' (1996: 51). It is also worth noting here that 'sexual difference is marked in the grammar' of the original French title of Derrida's *The Beast and the Sovereign* (*La bête et le souverain*) (2). Attending to the related questions of sexual difference and animality is important because it doubly undermines oppositional identity categories. As Kelly Oliver is right to point out: 'considering the various sexualities, sexes, and modes of sex among different animal species, not to mention the different individuals within species, might teach us to appreciate the multitude of sexualities and sexual differences beyond two' (2009: 148). In reading Derrida's texts, we find a deconstruction of sexual difference lurking in the shadows of the deconstructed human/animal binary.

The Animal That Therefore I Am ultimately demonstrates the importance of resisting homogeneous groupings of *the animal* and instead exploring *animals* in their multiplicity and heterogeneity. A necessary component of this insistence on heterogeneity is that animals cannot simply be equated with humans, which would mean 'ignoring or effacing everything that separates humankind from the other animals' (47). As this latter point suggests, Derrida doesn't intend to contradict 'the rupture or abyss' between humans and 'what we *call* animals'; he places 'heterogeneities and abyssal ruptures as against the homogeneous and the continuous' (30). And yet, despite emphasising that this abyssal rupture is not to be thought of as an 'indivisible line having two edges, Man and the Animal in general', the coupling of 'heterogeneities' and 'abyssal ruptures' is perhaps surprising. It implies that the choice is between on the one hand maintaining a distinction between humans and animals while exploring the heterogeneity of both, or on the other hand subverting the distinction and reducing everything to a homogeneity that erases difference entirely. The possibility that is overlooked in his own discussion is that of simultaneously subverting the 'abyss' between animal and human while still exploring heterogeneous differences. As Matthew Calarco argues in *Zoographies*, 'there is another option available':

> *we could simply let the human-animal distinction go* or, at the very least, not insist on maintaining it. Even if one agrees with Derrida that the task for thought is to attend to differences that have been overlooked and hidden by philosophical discourse, this does not mean that every difference and distinction that guides common sense and philosophy should be maintained and refined. Might not the challenge for philosophical thought today be to proceed altogether without the guardrails of the human-animal distinction and to invent new concepts and new practices along different paths? (2008: 149)

Calarco's call for creative theorising beyond dualism and binary oppositions may feel like a shortcut that bypasses the heavy philosophical burden of working through anthropocentric thought. It may even, however inadvertently, reinscribe the distinction it aims to subvert. For 'even if we decide', as John Llewelyn suggests, 'to avoid making this distinction in what we say, must we not, in order to carry out this resolution, retain the distinction in what we think?' (2010: 187). Nonetheless, Calarco reminds us that as well as critiquing the philosophical tradition the responsibility of animal theorists who want to respond to animal life is also to open up new pathways towards an affirmative future to think and enact life – whether human or nonhuman – together in all its heterogeneity.

For the Love of Dogs

The most frequently discussed pets in animal theory are undoubtedly dogs. As we saw in Chapter 2, Donna Haraway explores canine lives at the heart of her exploration of 'companion species' through a mixture of personal, philosophical and scientific story-telling. In *The Companion Species Manifesto* she writes that 'shaggy dog stories about evolution, love, training, and kinds or breeds' enable her to 'think about living well together with the host of species with whom human beings emerge on this planet at every scale of time, body, and space' (2003: 25). When Haraway speaks about domesticated animals, she is keen to avoid any sense of hierarchical relation. She wants to bring humans and animals into a more intimate material and conceptual entanglement, one which is not in any sense divided by an abyssal gulf. Rejecting the view that humans are somehow guilty of capturing and controlling pets, Haraway states: 'If I have a dog, my dog has a human; what that means concretely is at stake' (54). Echoing Montaigne, she inverts the expected hierarchy between human and pet and indicates a messier distribution of agency.

Haraway shares with Derrida an autobiographical focus, placing her own experiences at the heart of her encounter with animality. Like Derrida, Haraway also emphasises singular animals, but she does so with a difference. In *When Species Meet* she directly addresses the differences between her own theoretical approach, which continually returns to the 'mundane', everyday ways in which humans and animals are entangled (2008: 93), and Derrida's use of his cat to launch his theoretical exploration. Haraway begins her discussion of Derrida by acknowledging that he 'knew he was in the presence of someone, not of a machine' and, as a result, comes 'right to the edge of respect' for the animal (19–20). But Derrida's anti-Cartesian attitude towards his little cat is limited, according to Haraway, by his 'worries about being naked in front of his cat' and about the western philosophical tradition's treatment of the animal. 'Somehow in all this worrying and longing', writes Haraway, 'the cat was never heard from again . . . Derrida failed a simple obligation of companion species; he did not become curious about what the cat might actually be doing, feeling, thinking, or perhaps making available to him in looking back at him that morning' (20). What Haraway takes issue with here is that as much as Derrida's close textual analysis of western philosophy's own lack of curiosity about animals is important, he forgets the singular animal in front of him: 'Even if the cat did not become a symbol of all cats, the naked man's shame quickly became a figure for the shame of philosophy before all of the animals' (23). There is, however, something about Derrida's shameful response to his cat that cannot be characterised as a turning away from animality. In drawing attention to the shame of the philosopher, we should recall that Derrida originally presented the material about his cat as a lecture where he 'asks his audience, who are fast becoming his spectators, to view him as a body, and worse, as a *naked* body. In discussing his embarrassment at being embarrassed Derrida embarrasses himself' (Fudge 2007: 46). His reason for doing so is 'to undermine the arrogance he finds in the figure of the philosopher and in much philosophy . . . that has separated mind from body, and human from animal'. As Fudge points out, by setting the beginning of the discussion in the bathroom – 'a place of the body' – Derrida powerfully undermines the Cartesian 'I think therefore I am' that he is clearly taking aim at with the title of his work (46–7).

Haraway doesn't worry over shame in the way Derrida does. We can recall her cross-species kissing in Chapter 2 as a shameless (in the best possible sense) attempt to bring human and animal into a more intimate relation. If we are to respect and respond to the real lives of dogs (and other domesticated animals), Haraway argues, we should think of them less in terms of our 'pets' and more as 'significant others'. Breaking with the category of 'pet' is crucial if we are to foreground an always already historically, economically and ontologically entangled relationship where dogs have active and diverse roles to play in the world: 'dogs live in several twisted, braided categories at once; their biographies and their classifications are in a relation of torque'. In contrast to the word 'pet' which connotes servility, Haraway's 'companion species' not only captures this active role of dogs in their non-hierarchical relation to humans, but can also help to transform these relations. Naming takes on an ethical and ontological function in many facets of life, and where animals are concerned this is no different: 'changes in terminology can signal important mutations in the character of relationships – commercially, epistemologically, emotionally, and politically . . . "New" names mark changes in power, symbolically and materially remaking kin and kind' (2008: 135). So where Derrida, as described above, turns to the 'animot' to draw attention to the homogenising symbolic violence in the singular 'animal', Haraway turns to 'companionship' as a way to express the close bonds that tie human and nonhuman. Dogs are Haraway's case study for much broader cross-species entanglements, what she calls 'webbed bio-social-technical apparatuses of humans, animals, artifacts, and institutions in which particular ways of being emerge and are sustained. Or not' (134). Where Derrida's critique works from the inside of language and signification, Haraway pays more direct attention to material apparatuses.

A prominent example given by Haraway of non-hierarchical agential relations between companion species is that of agility training with her Australian Shepherd dog, Cayenne:

> Playing agility with Cayenne helps me understand a controversial, modern relationship between people and dogs: training to a high standard of performance for a competitive sport. Training together,

a particular woman and a particular dog, not Man and Animal in
the abstract, is a historically located multispecies, subject-shaping
encounter in a contact zone fraught with power, knowledge and
technique, moral questions – and the chance for joint, cross-species
invention that is simultaneously work and play. (205)

Once again we find an approach to theorising relations between human and
animal that makes use of concrete examples from everyday life. Agility training
provides Haraway with an example of domestic activity that doesn't fall into
the view of 'domestication of other sentient organisms as an ancient historical
disaster that has only grown worse over time' (206). Haraway is attentive to
how such a sport is embedded in socio-economic power structures – it is 'part
of globalized middle-class consumer cultures that can afford the considerable
time and money dedicated to the game' (207) – but argues that rather than
being about subjugation, agility training is a reciprocal teaching and learning

process between companion species in a 'contact zone' where 'the coming
into being of something unexpected' occurs (223). The actors involved in
the game are also 'unexpected': the 'who' that exists tied up in the knotting
of human-dog (or other animal) companionship 'refers to partners-in-the-
making through the active relations of coshaping, not to possessive human
or animal individuals whose boundaries and natures are set in advance of the
entanglements of becoming together' (206–7). The identities of the actors in
training emerge out of this encounter rather than already being pre-determined as 'human' and 'animal'.

Where the everyday interactions of companion species are concerned,
one of the most influential thinkers is Vicki Hearne. A dog and horse trainer
as well as theorist of human relations with domestic animals, Hearne seeks
to explore what she calls the 'rich and ever-changing web of philosophies
when good trainers talk and write' (2007: 3). Hearne's writings provide an
example of theory and practice meeting with the aim of finding new modes of
meaning-making and world-making. She argues in *Adam's Task* that we learn
how to be humble, respectful and caring humans precisely through the training of animals: 'trainers insist that training . . . results in ennoblement, in the
development of both the animal's *and the handler's* sense of responsibility and
honesty' (43). Certainly, Hearne succeeds in showing that in training 'the dog
is compellingly present' (44), while highlighting the ways in which trainers
are aware of the potential pitfalls of authority, the delicate balancing act about
what is *necessary* training, and the difference between correcting behaviour
and punishment. Getting the balance right is a challenge for relationships
between humans and animals, but also the relationships humans have with one
another – we all 'command' each other regularly (76). In *Animal Happiness*,
Hearne writes in some detail about how such commands come about from a

form of 'owning' and 'possessing' which is not about the dominance of one species over another, but is instead 'reciprocal, and even symmetrical to some degree' (1994: 207). For Hearne we utterly miss the reality of human-dog relations if we compare them to an act of slavery. Indeed, the ownership of dogs is the opposite of cruelty or dominance: 'it is more accurate to say that if I abuse my dog on the grounds that she is my dog, then I do not, at the moment at least, in fact own the dog, am not owning up to what goes into owning a dog' and, she adds, 'do not understand my own words when I say I own the dog' (208). When responsibility of ownership is emphasised, the training of animals becomes 'a human duty' (2007: 265).

In discussions of reciprocally trained companion species, however, the question remains as to whether the erasure of the term 'pet' in fact erases an important asymmetry, if not hierarchy, built into the relations between humans and domesticated animals. It may be true that on a macro (bio-socio-techno) and micro (familial) level dogs have been, and remain, active agents rather than passive recipients. Yet some of the examples theorists like Haraway and Hearne offer to highlight this canine agency are in danger of overlooking the actions imposed *upon* dogs. Even if we see dogs as themselves having agency, and even if Haraway and Hearne wouldn't in any way want to suggest that humans and dogs are exactly the same, neither seem to adequately take into account what is differently at stake for these human and nonhuman agents. We need to be careful not to train ourselves in reassurance regarding our relations with domestic animals to the point where we obscure the power dynamics implicit in the relation. For example, we might ask: do animals need to be trained to be happy? Could there be other forms of happiness, or ways of being where they might flourish? When Haraway writes of the 'laughter, tears, work, and play' she shared with her dog when agility training (2008: 208), there is, perhaps, a latent anthropocentrism (in not paying enough attention to the asymmetries in the co-shaping) and anthropomorphism (in projecting these human emotional characteristics onto dogs) at play. Training is undoubtedly a form of co-shaping, but we should also account for the qualitative differences in how actors shape and are shaped, and we should consider who decides what activity will lead to this co-shaping in the first place. What would happen if animals took the lead, so to speak, if we followed animals and were trained by them? Moreover, all the above inter-species encounters involved face-to-face, touch-to-touch, interactions that humans have with animals. Whereas, as Haraway herself notes, there is a more challenging question to address: 'what if the question of how animals engage *one another's* gaze *responsively* takes center stage for people?' (22). Training activities, and human-pet relations more broadly, cannot answer this question because in these domestic environments one thing that is always true is that a human is one of the actors.

Nonetheless, it is precisely because human life is already so entangled with animal life that accounting for our relations with pets is so important. To write off all dog ownership as a form of cruelty would be to put abstract principles *about* animals above concrete, everyday encounters *with* animals. Despite the relative limitations in the accounts provided by Derrida, Haraway and Hearne, it seems clear that companion animals have taken an active role in affecting how theorists approach the question of animality. Domestic animals have a privileged role for many animal theorists because they allow personal, emotional connections to spark a wider analysis of the relationship between nature and culture. As Haraway writes: 'To be in love means to be worldly, to be in connection with significant otherness and signifying others, on many scales, in layers of locals and globals' (97). In understanding the human relation to pets this attention to local and global levels is crucial in ensuring we don't just focus on personal relations with animals. It also counters those, like Francione and Berger, who see the love of pets as masking a wider indifference to, or even complicity in, the exploitation of animals. 'Dog love', as Marjorie Garber argues in her book of that title, 'is not an evasion or a substitution' but instead 'calls upon the same range and depth of feelings that humans have for humans' and has 'often brought out the best in us' (1996: 14–15). If we only think of dogs, cats and other domestic pets as human substitutes – even if such a critique is an important part of the story – we fail to take seriously the feelings we have for them and we miss the insight they have to offer us. Bringing out the best in our relations with companion animals means responding to the ways in which human and animal responses are entangled in our shared, everyday life.

PHENOMENOLOGICAL WORLDS

On a local and global scale, humans and animals are involved in multiple forms of world-making. As Haraway teaches us, 'species interdependence is the name of the worlding game on earth, and that game must be one of response and respect'. Given the wide variety of this worldly play – which includes 'technologies, commerce, organisms, landscapes, peoples, practices' (2008: 19) – how can we respond with respect to animal worlds? We can't easily claim that all experiences of worldly encounters are the same, whether those involved share a domestic dwelling or not. Nor is it easy to speak about one 'world' that humans and animals all inhabit. How then do we understand this term 'world' in relation to animals and animality? In what ways can we speak about distinct human worlds and animal worlds? To what extent can humans know animal worlds and to what extent can animals know human worlds? Such questions concerning the meaning of the term 'world', and how the relationship between humans and animals affects our understanding of how the world is experienced, are crucial for animal theorists. It would be too simple to say that responding with respect to animals is a matter of welcoming them into our human world; the truly respectful response would be in following the animal's lead in an effort to reconceptualise what that 'world' is.

Concrete, everyday experience meets with this more abstract idea of worlds in phenomenological approaches to animal life. Consider the following passage, taken from the second volume of Edmund Husserl's pivotal work, *Ideas Pertaining to a Pure Phenomenology and to a Phenomenological Philosophy*. Husserl, the founder of phenomenology at the beginning of the twentieth century, here draws humans and animals together in his discussion of two ways of thinking about the natural world: first, 'nature in a more strict sense, the lowest and first sense, i.e., material *nature*'; second, nature in the 'broadened sense, i.e., things that have a soul, in the genuine sense of "living," *animal nature*'. It is this second form of nature that animals share with humans:

> Everything that we take as existing in the ordinary sense (thus in a naturalistic attitude), including therefore, sensations, representations, feelings, and psychic acts and states of every kind, belongs precisely in this attitude to living nature; these are 'real' acts or states, ontologically characterized precisely in that they are activities or states of animals or humans and as such are part of the spatio-temporal world. (1989: 31)

Husserl points to how both human and nonhuman animals have a physical and psychic relation to the world. They are 'Bodies with soul' – with soul here standing for the principle of life rather than a religious entity – (35) and they are both, as Corinne Painter puts it, 'constituted by a stream of consciousness that hangs together in such a way as to identify the animal and the human as the self-same psych-physical entity that it is' (2007: 98). There is the potential here to begin to think about the ways in which everyday, concrete realities of human and nonhuman animals reveal a shared 'life-world' as Husserl goes on to call it (1989: 384–5). But while Husserl writes more fully about this key concept of the 'life-world, or the world of original experience' in texts such as *The Crisis of European Sciences and Transcendental Phenomenology* (1970: 227), it is his followers, Martin Heidegger and Maurice Merleau-Ponty, who more explicitly, and in diverging manners, address the place of animals in the world.

Poverty in World

In *The Fundamental Concepts of Metaphysics*, the published version of a lecture course given in 1929–30, Heidegger frames his discussion of 'man' and 'animal' around the question 'What is world?' (1995: 176). He goes on to compare the relation of different forms of life to the world:

man is not merely a *part of the world* but is also master and servant of the
world in the sense of '*having*' world. Man has world. But then what about
the other beings which, like man, are also part of the world: the animals
and plants, the material things like the stone, for example? Are they
merely parts of the world, as distinct from man who in addition *has* world?
Or does the animal too have world, and if so, in what way? In the same way
as man, or in some other way? And how would we grasp this otherness?
And what about the stone? However crudely, certain distinctions
immediately manifest themselves here. We can formulate these
distinctions in the following three theses: [1.] the stone (material object) is
worldless; [2.] the animal is *poor in world*; [3.] man is *world-forming*. (177)

Based on this passage alone we would think that Heidegger is setting up a
simple hierarchical framework in which to distinguish man, animal and stone.
Although it is often interpreted in this way when read in isolation, it is crucial
to remember that this passage is only his starting point for working through
issues relating to animal worlds. Heidegger is deeply interested in the question of animal life, as can be seen by his extensive discussion and unpacking
of these terms over the remainder of his lecture series. And while the stone
remains something that is absolutely without world – that is, without access to
the world – a more nuanced discussion emerges in relation to animals and their
distinction from humans.

The animal takes a central role in Heidegger's theorising precisely because
he wants to avoid a naive categorical schema 'which assumes that we are
dealing with three beings all present at hand in exactly the same way' (202).
He explains that the 'essence of the animal' and its relation to the world is of
primary importance in uncovering not only the difference between 'man' and
'animal' but also in reaching a more precise concept of 'world' (185–6). What
Heidegger means by the distinction between poor in world and world-forming
is not a quantitative or even qualitative difference that would place life in some
kind of hierarchical order of 'completeness':

this comparison between man and animal, characterized in terms
of world-formation and poverty in world respectively, allows no
evaluative ranking or assessment with respect to completeness or
incompleteness . . . The questionable character of this approach also
affects the judgements we make within the animal realm itself. Here
too we are accustomed to speaking about higher and lower animals, but
it is nevertheless a fundamental mistake to suppose that amoebae or
infusoria are more imperfect or incomplete animals than elephants or
apes. Every animal and every species of animal as such is just as perfect
and complete as any other. (194)

If we are to respect the multitude of species that inhabit the world then we cannot claim that one animal is 'more imperfect or incomplete' than another animal or indeed human.

In order to consider distinctions between humans and animals Heidegger instead turns to a discussion of the *accessibility* of the objective world. Two important examples are presented, which centre on lizards and bees. Firstly, he describes a lizard who 'basks in the sun' by placing itself on a stone. Heidegger claims that the lizard does not relate to the stone or sun in the same way as the human would conceptualise and relate to these material objects 'as' stone and sun. But at the same time the lizard does have some access to the material world, unlike the stone that has 'no possible access to anything else around it' (197). The lizard's experience of the world cannot then be conflated with the experience of either humans or objects: it has a distinct 'relation to the rock, to the sun, and to a host of other things. One is tempted to suggest that what we identify as the rock and the sun are just lizard-things for the lizard, so to speak.' As a result, Heidegger suggests that 'when we say that the lizard is lying on the rock, we ought to cross out the word "rock" in order to indicate that whatever the lizard is lying on is certainly given *in some way* for the lizard, and yet is not known to the lizard *as a rock*' (198). In turning to bees in a second example, Heidegger draws on an experiment by Czech biologist Emanuel Rádl that showed how bees use the sun to orientate their flight paths and navigate their way back to their hives: 'The bee is simply given over to the sun and to the period of its flight without being able to grasp either of these as such, without being able to reflect upon them as something thus grasped' (247). Heidegger's claim about the bee's relation to the world shares similarities with Lacan's view of how bee activity relates to language (for Lacan, as discussed in Chapter 1, the bee's mode of communication is of a different register from the symbolic order of the human). Whether lizard, bee, or any other nonhuman creature, Heidegger argues that the lack of a relation to the external world 'as such' means that the animal's experience is of a different order entirely to the human: 'it is *not* simply a question of a *qualitative otherness* of the animal world as compared with the human world, and especially not a question of quantitative distinctions in range, depth, and breadth'. Instead, the question becomes more profoundly 'whether the animal can apprehend something *as* something, something *as* a being, at all' (264).

Heidegger distinguishes the essence of animality by focusing on the 'captivation' of the animal. This is not to be understood as a sense of imprisonment in the same way a human would experience it, because the animal never experiences a freedom that is taken away in captivation – it is 'essentially captivated' by being 'absorbed in itself':

Captivation is not some state that accompanies the animal, into which it sometimes temporarily falls, nor is it a state in which it simply finds

itself permanently. It is the inner possibility of animal being itself
. . . We do not regard captivation as a state that merely accompanies
behaviour, but as the inner possibility of behaviour as such. (239)

Heidegger then shifts from discussing an animal relation to the 'world' to what
he calls a 'disinhibiting ring' that conditions behaviour. The animal 'surrounds
itself with a disinhibiting ring which prescribes what can affect or occasion its
behaviour' (255). This disinhibiting ring is not a description of 'some invisible field radiating around the animal at its center' where everything that falls
within its reach is accessible; rather, animals are at first 'inhibited in their relations such that only select beings may penetrate and disinhibit their behaviour'
(Buchanan 2008: 93–4). If the disinhibiting ring should be understood as 'a
continual openness for whatever manifests itself to the animal in its environment' (McNeill 1999: 222), then it is crucial to remember that what manifests
itself is limited to only certain beings. Instead of judging animals' access to the
world on the same terms as he does humans', Heidegger attempts to understand how the world, or 'ring', the animal experiences is distinctive. While he
is often thought of as providing a negative definition of animal experience as
that which is *lesser* than human experience, Heidegger actually aims in these
lectures to forge a positive conception of the essence of animality where what
he initially called 'poverty' is actually 'a kind of wealth' (Heidegger 1995: 255).
Each animal has its own disinhibiting ring, its own different mode of captivation, and so only from an anthropocentric angle could we judge the animal as
being 'poor' in what we usually think of as 'world'.

Animal Umwelten

Heidegger is influenced in *The Fundamental Concepts of Metaphysics* by the
Estonian-German biologist and ethologist Jakob von Uexküll, whose theory of
the 'Umwelt' (or 'environment-world' as it is sometimes translated) has been
an important consideration among philosophers who have followed Heidegger
in theorising animal worlds. Heidegger's comment above about how 'every
species of animal as such is just as perfect and complete as any other' shares
similarities with Uexküll's theory of multiple Umwelten which posits that
'all animal subjects, from the simplest to the most complex, are inserted into
their environments to the same degree of perfection. The simple animal has a
simple environment; the multiform animal has an environment just as richly
articulated as it is' (Uexküll 2010: 50). Uexküll's work – and Heidegger is
referring mainly to *The Environment and Inner World of Animals*, written in
1909 – is described in *The Fundamental Concepts of Metaphysics* as a decisive
step in biology in that it provides insight into how 'the animal is bound to its
environment' (Heidegger 1995: 261). In doing so, Heidegger argues, Uexküll

offers a more nuanced view of the relation of animals to their environments than Darwinists of the time could offer:

> In Darwinism such investigations were based upon the fundamentally misconceived idea that the animal is present at hand, and then subsequently adapts itself to a world that is present at hand, that it then comports itself accordingly and that the fittest individual gets selected. Yet the task is not simply to identify the specific conditions of life materially speaking, but rather to acquire insight into the relational structure between the animal and its environment. (263)

Seeing the animal and the environment as two distinct entities that happen to come together, Darwinism doesn't pay enough attention to their intimate 'relational structure' (Buchanan 2008: 48).

A Foray into the Worlds of Animals and Humans, published a few years after Heidegger's lectures, collects Uexküll's thoughts on over twenty years of Umwelt research. In it, he provides a further example of animal worlding by using the metaphor of the 'soap bubble' which echoes the idea of a disinhibiting ring:

> We must therefore imagine all the animals that animate Nature around us, be they beetles, butterflies, gnats, or dragonflies who populate a meadow, as having a soap bubble around them, closed on all sides, which closes off their visual space and in which everything visible for the subject is also enclosed . . . Only when we can vividly imagine this fact will we recognise in our own world the bubble that encloses each and every one of us on all sides. (Uexküll 2010: 69)

Uexküll's account of nonhuman and human animal worlds emphasises their different range of experiences, and warns against enclosing the animal's perceptual world within our own. For Uexküll 'there is no space independent of subjects', and these subjects include nonhuman animals. Any human concept of a holistic, 'all-encompassing world-space' is an anthropocentric 'fiction' or 'fable' (70). As Giorgio Agamben – who in *The Open* describes Uexküll as 'one of the greatest zoologists of the twentieth century' (2004: 39) – explains:

> There does not exist a forest as an objectively fixed environment: there exists a forest-for-the-park-ranger, a forest-for-the-hunter, a forest-for-the-botanist, a forest-for-the-wayfarer, a forest-for-the-nature-lover, a forest-for-the-carpenter . . . Even a minimal detail – for example, the stem of a wildflower – when considered as a carrier of significance, constitutes a different element each time it is in a different environment. (41)

Because of the different phenomenological experiences of different creatures, it makes little sense to talk of one 'world' that humans and animals differently navigate – they are, in fact, navigating different worldly dimensions. We might read Heidegger's description above of 'lizard things for the lizard' in precisely this way.

But if we look more closely at Uexküll's work a significant difference emerges in comparison to Heidegger. That is, Uexküll places greater emphasis on each animal's creative and *meaningful* relations to their environment. Development, as Uexküll stresses in his 1940 text *A Theory of Meaning*, is non-linear and contains a fundamentally different meaning based on different animals. In the natural world we find

> hundreds of variations, but never showing any transitions from the imperfect to the perfect. Environments were certainly simpler at the beginning of the world-drama than they were later. But, in them, each carrier of meaning faced a recipient of meaning. Meaning ruled them all. Meaning bound changing organs to the changing medium . . . Everywhere there was progression, but nowhere progress in the sense of the survival of the fittest, never a selection of the better by a planlessly raging battle for existence. (2010: 196)

The meaning derived from animal Umwelten is ascertained through the animal's ability to discern what aspects of its surroundings help it to function, or what objects are of significance to it. Uexküll firmly rejects the mechanistic model of animal behaviour, which Heidegger's discussion of lizards and bees can sometimes fall into. What is emphasised is that meaning-making – and therefore a kind of world-forming – is not restricted to the human's cultural realm: '*The question as to meaning must therefore have priority in all living beings*' (2010: 151). We might even say that Uexküll is more willing than Heidegger to consider the animal's relation to its environment 'as such'.

For Heidegger, Uexküll's willingness to discuss the shared manner in which humans and animals meaningfully relate to their environments is precisely what limits his approach: firstly, in Uexküll's work 'world' and 'subject' are under-theorised terms; and secondly, Uexküll doesn't adequately account for the humans' ability to transcend their own Umwelten (Heidegger 1995: 263–4). In contrast to Uexküll, Heidegger's nuanced probing of the concept of 'world', and his unwillingness to judge animal experience on the same terms as human experience, offers the potential for a more philosophically rigorous non-anthropocentric and non-anthropomorphic approach to animal life. And yet, there remains something unsatisfying about the very manner in which Heidegger dismisses the possibility of animals relating to their environment 'as such'. To be sure, Heidegger does make clear that the thesis that the animal is poor in world 'is misleading precisely with respect to the essence of animality itself' in that 'it encourages the mistaken view that the being of the animal in itself is intrinsically deprivation and poverty'. He concludes that his 'thesis that the animal is poor in world is accordingly far from being a, let alone the, fundamental metaphysical principle of the essence of animality' and is instead the consequence of a comparative methodology of distinguishing human and animal (271). But in attempting to provide the pathway to a non-anthropocentric and non-anthropomorphic view Heidegger's reasoning suggests an even greater, more profound experience of poverty in the animal's experience of its environment. In not considering that some relation to the 'as such' may be possible, he asserts that 'the animal is separated from man by an abyss' (264). The comparison between 'the animal' and 'man' – and it is perhaps convenient that Heidegger turns for his examples to insects and tiny creatures who more obviously differ in form from humans than, say, other mammals – frequently leaves us with a sense that animal relations with their environments are pre-set and 'purely instinctual' (248). Because human and animal have, for Heidegger, different essences, we are discouraged from thinking of animals as either *forming* their own worlds or *sharing* a world with humans.

However promising Heidegger's analysis appears, he ends up distinguishing humans and animals not only in life but also in death. In a later section of *The Fundamental Concepts of Metaphysics*, he writes of how animals don't have access to death 'as such': 'Because captivation belongs to the essence of the animal, the animal cannot die in the sense in which dying is ascribed to human beings but can only come to an end' (267). If the animal's world holds it in 'captivation', and if this is the 'essence of the animal', it has no ability to know, conceive or experience what is outside of that world. In ontologically trapping the animal in its world it is also easier to ignore ethical responsibilities towards those we see as not under threat of dying in the same way that humans are. The implication is, as Paola Cavalieri argues, that animals can be 'lightheartedly killed' because they 'merely perish' (2009: 11). There is also the problematic assumption that humans *do* know what it is like to die as such. Derrida seeks to unsettle such beliefs in *The Beast and the Sovereign*: 'it's not at all certain in any case that man has a relation to death or an experience of death *as such*, in its possible impossibility, or', he adds, 'that one can say, properly, in the proper sense and simply, calmly, that the animal is deprived of it' (2009: 308). Although, as discussed above, Derrida asserts his own 'abyss' between humans and animals, he maintains an openness towards the multiple world-making capacities of animals just as he here remains open to the experience of dying that may or may not be available to humans and nonhumans. Heidegger, in comparison, is too quick to draw lines between the lives and deaths that matter.

The Flesh of the World

Later phenomenological attempts to engage with animal Umwelten adopt a different approach to Heidegger's. The emphasis Uexküll's theory of Umwelten places on multiple experiences of the world influenced the French phenomenologist Maurice Merleau-Ponty, and this is most evident in his *Nature* courses given between 1956 and 1960, and in his unfinished book *The Visible and the Invisible*, published in French in 1964 three years after his death. What is particularly significant about Uexküll's impact on Merleau-Ponty's thought is that it contributed to a move away from an approach whereby phenomenology was predominantly concerned with human consciousness and experience. Merleau-Ponty takes the groundwork laid by Husserl and Heidegger a step further and forges an ontology that entangles human and animal life. In the words of Brett Buchanan, who in *Onto-Ethologies* offers a fine analysis of how both Heidegger and Merleau-Ponty engage Uexküll's studies: 'whereas Heidegger uses the *Umwelt* as the basis for considering the ontological differences between animal environments and human world, Merleau-Ponty's interest is directed more to how its melodic undertone parallels a theory of nature overall'. Merleau-Ponty is less interested in distinctions between human and animal and more so in 'immediate participation between humans and animals in the same source of life' (2008: 147).

Signs of Merleau-Ponty's interest in animals appear in *The World of Perception*, his radio lectures from 1948. In the fourth lecture in the series, on 'Animal Life', Merleau-Ponty writes about the openness of the world of perception – that is, the world of the senses rediscovered by phenomenology – to animals:

> the way we relate to the things of the world is no longer as a pure intellect trying to master an object or space that stands before it. Rather, this relationship is an ambiguous one, between beings who are both embodied and limited and an enigmatic world . . . this world is not just open to other human beings but also to animals, children, primitive peoples and madmen who dwell in it after their own fashion; they too coexist in this world. Today we shall see that the rediscovery of the world of perception allows us to find greater meaning and interest in these extreme or aberrant forms of life and consciousness. (2008: 54)

While we might query the implication of terminology that includes animals among 'children, primitive peoples and madmen' as 'aberrant' and not 'human beings', Merleau-Ponty is critical of how we have for so long considered those not 'healthy' and 'normal' through what they lacked, or what they were incapable of. As a result, we have failed to consider the other modes of world-making that might be part of their under-appreciated capabilities. Like so many of the animal theorists explored in this book, he is critical of the Cartesian judgement of beings as either human or machine (54–5). But it would be wrong to suggest that Merleau-Ponty here endows animals with exactly the same world-forming capacities as humans. He is clear that the animal – and like Heidegger it is often a singular, homogenised 'animal' that is under discussion in this lecture – engages 'a process of "giving shape" to the world' (59). However, he describes this process as 'trial and error', whereby the animal navigates 'its surroundings in a manner consistent with the laws of a sort of naive physics'. He adds that the animal 'has at best a meagre capacity to accumulate knowledge' and is thrown into 'a world to which it has no key' (58–9). Nonetheless, Merleau-Ponty insists that rather than assuming the human is the pinnacle of existence and possesses a boundless capacity for knowledge, humans must be aware of their limitations and remain open to other experiences of the world, including those of animals. 'We will only see this', he argues, 'if we lend our attention to the spectacle of the animal world, if we are prepared to live alongside the world of animals instead of rashly denying it any kind of interiority' (58).

Merleau-Ponty's discussion of animal worlds becomes more detailed, and explicitly refers to Uexküll, in his later work. In the *Nature* courses, he opens the section on 'Animality: The Study of Animal Behaviour' with an extended discussion of Uexküll. Like Heidegger, Merleau-Ponty expresses dissatisfaction with a Darwinian approach to animal life where 'different fortuitous elements are welded together because every other arrangement, or at least every bad arrangement, would not explain the survival of the animal' (2003: 175). Where Darwinians (and often the disagreement is with interpretations by Darwin's followers more than Darwin's writings themselves) focus on the 'extraordinary arrangements' that mean certain species 'were able to survive', Merleau-Ponty follows Uexküll in claiming that this focus on survival of the fittest 'suppresses' the way that animals with less extraordinary arrangements are still perfectly adapted to their environment:

> Each action of the milieu is conditioned by the action of the animal; the animal's behaviour arouses responses from the milieu. There is an action in return for that made by the animal, which returns to the behavior of the animal. In brief, the exterior and the interior, the situation and the movement are not in a simple relation of causality. (175)

Merleau-Ponty's view of animality here is less focused on hard-wired mechanised processes and more on context-dependent, meaningful movements: 'The *Umwelt* is less and less oriented toward a goal and more and more toward the interpretation of symbols.' The animal becomes an active participant in a nature which contains 'a beginning of culture' (176). More concerned with connections between human and nonhuman than what separates them, Merleau-Ponty finds in the Umwelt a theory of 'life as the opening of a field of action', an opening onto an 'inter-animality' that connects beings within species and between different species (173).

As the *Nature* courses unfold Merleau-Ponty introduces a discussion of 'the flesh of the world' (216), a concept that evades clean distinctions between subject and object, interior and exterior, embodiment and environment. Our bodies become central to an openness to the world: 'instead of a science of the world by relations contemplated from the outside (relations of space, for example), the body is the measurement of the world. I am open to the world because I am *within* my body' (217). This statement does not mean that the body encloses an individual being set against the backdrop of the world; rather, Merleau-Ponty conceptualises 'the body as open totality . . . The flesh of the body makes us understand the flesh of the world' (218). Where Heidegger's exploration of the Umwelt led to distinctions between *different orders* of world between human and animal, Merleau-Ponty outlines a pulsing, creative world that is the *shared* setting of all life: 'The point is not to argue that being human is the same as being every other sort of animal, but that all manners of life partake in the whole of natural ontology' (Buchanan 2008: 147). As such, Merleau-Ponty begins to outline a conception of the world that is, as Louise Westling suggests in *The Logos of the Living World*, 'a radical challenge to anthropocentric arrogance' and that returns humanity to an inter-species community of life (Westling 2014: 5).

Merleau-Ponty develops this notion of 'the flesh of the world' more fully in *The Visible and the Invisible*, where the primary focus on consciousness in early phenomenology gives way to the beginnings of a new ontology of nature. Even further removed from Cartesian dualism, human consciousness is no longer placed before animal embodiment in describing our relations with the world:

> between the knowledge of self and the knowledge of the world there is
> no longer any debate over even ideal priority. In particular the world is
> no longer *founded on* the 'I think,' as the bound on the binding. What
> I 'am' I am only at a distance, yonder, in this body, this personage,
> these thoughts, which I push before myself and which are only my least
> remote distances . . . and conversely I adhere to this world which is not
> me as closely as to myself, in a sense it is only the prolongation of my
> body – I am justified in saying that I am in the world. Idealism and the
> reflective cramp disappear because the relation of knowledge is based
> on a 'relation of being,' because for me to be is not to remain in identity,
> it is to bear before myself the identifiable, *what there is*, to which I add
> nothing but the tiny doublet 'such as it is.' (1968: 57)

The human is part of an 'ontological vibration' (115), where our starting point for understanding being-in-the-world is not the human mind, but our embodied openness to nature: 'all we must do is situate ourselves within the being we are dealing with, instead of looking at it from the outside – or, *what amounts to the same thing*, what we have to do is put it back into the fabric of our life' (117). Merleau-Ponty moves between the equally troubling poles of dogmatic idealism and materialism, claiming that 'it would be naive to seek solidarity in a heaven of ideas or in a *ground* (*fond*) of meaning – it is neither above nor beneath the appearances, but at their joints; it is the tie that secretly connects an experience to its variants' (116). Crucially, he doesn't want to erase the gaps that exist between different 'living bodies', but at the same time he does want to stress 'cohesion between living things' (Buchanan 2008: 132). Merleau-Ponty therefore conceptualises the simultaneous *variations* and *connections* through which life unfolds.

The 'joints' that are the new foundation of life are the shared unfolding of nature. The body does not belong to a self-enclosed human subject but is part of 'a *flesh* of things': 'the body belongs to the order of the things as the world is universal flesh' (1968: 133; 137). It is important to underline what Merleau-Ponty does *not* mean by this word 'flesh': firstly, it 'is not matter' (139; 146); and secondly, it is not part of a transcendent, mystical schema. It is, rather, a kind of '"element" of being' – in the sense that water, air, earth and fire are thought of as elements – which 'has no name in any philosophy' (139; 147). Flesh doesn't, then, start from 'substances' that belong to the subjective or objective world; the flesh of the world is primary, it is a 'wild or brute being' that signals the always already intertwined nature of human and nonhuman, material and immaterial, visible and invisible (211): 'That means that my body is made of the same flesh as the world . . . and moreover that this flesh of my body is shared by the world, the world *reflects* it, encroaches upon it and it encroaches upon the world . . . they are in a relation of transgression or of overlapping.' Merleau-Ponty finds in the body a 'measurement' of 'all the dimensions of the world' (248). While *The Visible and the Invisible* doesn't explore a specifically 'animal' life at any great length, this is because it moves firmly away from a Heideggerian language of different 'essences' of human and animal and their respective abilities to access the world. The flesh of the world describes a primordial intercorporeality open to *all* life.

WHY NOT AN OLFACTORY ART? *TIMBUKTU*

Attempts to express animal life in literature are so often focused on the worlds of pets, and frequently the chosen species is the dog. Such writings about domestic animals can illustrate the vital role they play in the everyday lives of humans and can complicate the hierarchical divides between human and animal in a similar way to Derrida and Haraway. But they can also reveal the problems associated with pet ownership, including the ways in which domestic animals are mistreated. Moreover, while many nonhuman animals in novels find themselves in the background of the main plot, casting a dog in the role of protagonist provides an opportunity to imagine specifically canine phenomenological experiences of the world and therefore to explore the kinds of issues raised by Heidegger and Merleau-Ponty. But while the very questions about pets and their experiences of the world that are raised by animal theorists can be found in literature, there is a key difference: instead of thinking about animals and how they relate to the world, we find attempts to represent the way *an animal* thinks about the world. In the process the role of language comes under greater scrutiny, for words are used to directly express the consciousness and everyday experience of a canine protagonist who is more often concerned with smell than the sound of human voices.

Paul Auster's 1999 novel *Timbuktu* offers a playful but also serious exploration of a dog's life. Mr Bones, as the canine protagonist is named, provides an example of the 'vast menagerie of philosophizing animals in today's literature' (Ittner 2006: 91). He is, it becomes clear, a thinking dog. Auster writes the story of Mr Bones' journey with his master Willy from Brooklyn to Baltimore, followed by Willy's death and supposed journey to the afterlife, 'Timbuktu', which leaves Mr Bones – who we find grieving, remembering and even dreaming – to try to find a new home. In the process the novel reveals both the pitfalls of exploiting dogs within their domestic arenas, as well as the potential ways in which thinking with dogs might allow for a different perspective on life. In just the second paragraph the narrator emphasises the connection between Willy and Mr Bones as he worries over Willy's demise:

> Mr. Bones had been with Willy since his earliest days as a pup, and by now it was next to impossible for him to imagine a world that did not have his master in it. Every thought, every memory, every particle of the earth and air was saturated with Willy's presence. Habits die hard, and no doubt there's some truth to the adage about old dogs and new tricks, but it was more than just love or devotion that caused Mr. Bones to dread what was coming. It was pure ontological terror. Subtract Willy from the world, and the odds were that the world itself would cease to exist. (Auster 1999: 4)

Here we see both the dependency of dogs on humans where Mr Bones' human 'master' is synonymous with the world, but also the profound and intimate emotional and molecular entanglement that 'saturated' their existence. The phrase 'pure ontological terror' perfectly captures this intertwined life which both consigns the dog to human rule but enables their shared modes of being.

Auster more liberally describes the mind of the animal than we saw Carter do in Chapter 1, appearing to worry less about the problems associated with anthropomorphism. One advantage of detailing long passages of Mr Bones' thoughts, feelings and even dreams is that it urges readers to question that which has previously not been thought worth questioning. *Timbuktu* takes for granted that dogs do think and feel so as to explore the more interesting question of *how* and *what* they think, *how* and *what* they feel. Auster's efforts to probe these questions should therefore be seen as an experiment where human language is used to *theorise* what it is like to make sense of the world as a dog. We see this in the relationship between Mr Bones and Willy, where the latter is genuinely interested in 'dogness' and 'canine habits':

> until Mr Bones came into his life, he had never had the opportunity
> to observe a dog's behaviour at close hand, had never even bothered to
> give the subject much thought. Dogs were no more than dim presences
> to him, shadowy figures hovering at the edge of consciousness. You
> avoided the ones who barked at you, you patted the ones who licked
> you. That was the extent of his knowledge. Two months after his
> thirty-eighth birthday, all that suddenly changed.
> There was so much to absorb, so much evidence to assimilate,
> decipher, and make sense of that Willy hardly knew where to begin.
> The wagging tail as opposed to the tail between the legs. The pricked
> ears as opposed to the flaccid ears. The rolling on to the back, the
> running in circles, the anus-sniffs and growls, the kangaroo-hops and
> midair turns, the stalking crouch, the bared teeth, the cocked head,
> and a hundred other minute particulars, each one an expression of a
> thought, a feeling, a plan, an urge. It was like learning how to speak a
> new language. (37)

Here Willy tries to recognise and respond to Mr Bones' distinct form of world-making. He attends to 'minute particulars' that shift the dog from the 'edge of consciousness' to the centre of thought. Dog capacities, usually viewed as instinctive reactions, are instead considered as meaningful bodily articulations of 'a thought, a feeling, a plan, an urge'. Therefore, while Auster's narrator must use language to depict this dog's life, the crucial point is that his character Willy shows an awareness of another kind of experience that he himself struggles to access. Contained in a simile – 'It was like learning a new language' – this canine world-making is connected to the human world of language but cannot be reduced to it; the focus is turned from what a dog lacks to what a human lacks.

The different register of canine world-forming is presented through the focus on smell: 'For true knowledge, for a genuine grasp of reality in all its manifold configurations, only the nose was of any value' (38). Mr Bones has a seemingly 'boundless' capacity to make meaning out of smell; it is an ability that shows dogs have different worlds from humans, even if they are also entangled in human life: 'A dog had roughly two hundred and twenty million scent receptors, whereas a man had but five million.' With such a quantitative 'disparity', 'it was logical to assume that the world perceived by a dog was quite different from the one perceived by a man'. Rather than seeing this dog as deprived because it cannot access objects 'as such', the novel here wonders about those experiences of the world the human is deprived of. This includes a consideration of whether the human has access to objects 'as such' if we take smell as the privileged sense rather than speech: 'What did Mr. Bones experience when he smelled something? And, just as important, why did he smell what he smelled?' (39). Smell is not, then, theorised as something that allows the dog to merely navigate its surroundings; instead, this sense provides a rich and meaningful experience of life. In a strikingly original series of questions – we read that 'no one had ever thought of this before'– we are even asked to consider whether smell could create its own aesthetics: 'who was to say they wouldn't respond to an art based on the sense of smell? Why not an olfactory art? Why not an art for dogs that dealt with the world as dogs knew it?' (40–1). If the 'question of the animal' that is under scrutiny by animal theorists must necessarily open up rather than close down questions as to animal life in both domestic and worldly arenas, then here Auster's novel does precisely that. Willy asks: 'What was the ideal sequence of smells? How long should a symphony last, and how many smells should it contain?' (41). Not only do such questions ask us to consider canine worlds on their own terms, they also self-reflexively comment on the limitations of this very novel, which relies wholly on words to communicate its meaning. In posing these questions, *Timbuktu* emphasises a shared sympathy (or, we might say, 'symphony') between human and dog while pointing to two very different experiences of the world. Here we find an intimate entanglement of human and pet, and at the same time a respect for the asymmetrical ways in which they enter this entanglement.

But having pets doesn't always lead to the kind of imaginative and respectful responses that we find in Willy's relationship with Mr Bones. In *Timbuktu* we are also presented with the darker side of this uneven encounter between human and dog after Willy has died and Mr Bones seeks a new home. The inequality between species is emphasised in the way that Mr Bones, who as a domesticated dog is dependent on humans for his survival, appears to become willingly subservient. 'In his calmest, most self-assured manner' he allows a boy, Tiger, to find him and 'cling to him, patiently bearing the brunt of the tyke's phenomenal strength' – in other words, another human is needed to fill the void that had previously been saturated by Willy (126–7). In the first instance this new family treat him well, providing him with food so that 'he ate in a trance of contentment', and washing him in order to free his coat of ticks (130; 133–4). However, when the father, Dick, returns home, he lays down the law with the aim of asserting his human superiority over this dog. He dictates that the dog can stay on a trial basis so long as the following rules are adhered to:

> First: under no circumstances was the dog to be allowed in the house. Second: he would have to be taken to the vet for a full checkup. If he wasn't found to be in reasonably good health, he would have to go. Third: at the earliest possible convenience, an appointment would have to be made with a professional groomer. The dog needed a haircut, a shampoo, and a manicure, as well as a thorough going-over for ticks, lice, and fleas. Fourth: he would have to be fixed. And fifth: Alice would be responsible for feeding him and changing his water bowl – with no allowance for services rendered. (141–2)

Certain items on this list – notably the matter of cleaning and of feeding – had previously been taken up by the mother and Alice. But while they looked after Mr Bones with care and in response to his needs, Dick's orders are more concerned with a wish to assert both his patriarchal and human authority.

One of the most troubling rules on the list is that the dog shouldn't be allowed in the house: Mr Bones 'failed to grasp how a dog could become part of a family's household if he didn't have the right to enter that family's house'. Here we see a rejection of what makes a pet a domestic animal: namely, that it enters the human familial arena. This dog's marginalisation is emphasised in the fact he is not even allowed to be captive in the family home. Additionally, Dick is wholly unwilling to imagine the dog's capacities in the way that Willy had: '"Don't feel sorry for him, Alice. he's not a person, he's a dog, and dogs don't ask questions. They make do with what they get"' (142). And yet, undermining this assumption, Auster's protagonist *does* ask questions:

> Was this what life was going to be like around here?, he wondered. Were they simply going to abandon him in the morning and expect him to fend for himself all day? It felt like an obscene joke. He was a dog built for companionship, for the give-and-take of life with others, and he needed to be touched and spoken to, to be part of a world that included more than just himself . . . They had turned him into a prisoner. (144)

The difference between Willy and Dick in their treatment of the dog is that the former allows his canine companion to alter him and become truly entangled

in the 'give-and-take of life', whereas the latter fails to embrace any different form of life. Despite both sharing phallic names, it is Dick, rather than
Willy, who always wants to erect barriers between man and dog (and in the
process removes Mr Bones' sexual organs by taking him to be 'fixed' [151–2]).
Emphasising the victory of Dick's rule, the dog goes on to accept his subjugation in the modern family of late capitalist, consumerist society: he now
experienced 'the America of two-car garages, home-improvement vans, and
neo-Renaissance shopping malls' and 'he had no objections . . . once you got
used to the mechanics of the system, it no longer seemed so important that you
were tethered to a wire all day' (162–3). Mr Bones is captured by the mechanics of contemporary America, himself becoming a kind of machine emptied of
the vitality he shared with Willy – indeed Mr Bones dreams of Willy chastising
him for turning into 'a tired and disgusting joke' (172).

We are not to simply conclude that with Dick Mr Bones is captured and
without him he is free. In exploring different relationships between hominid
and canid *Timbuktu* exposes this choice of capture or escape as a false dichot-
omy. Consider the fact that when Mr Bones does escape patriarchal familial
rule – running away from the 'canine hotel' he is left in while the family are
enjoying a holiday in Disney World – he opts for death. Utterly dependent on humans for survival, he has no place to go other than the 'last turn'
of the imagined afterlife of 'Timbuktu . . . where dogs talked as equals with
men':

> All he had to do was step into the road . . . But Mr. Bones wasn't
> proposing anything as vulgar as suicide. He was merely going to play
> a game . . . Just run across the road and see if you could avoid being
> hit. The more times you were able to do it, the greater the champion
> you were. Sooner or later, of course, the odds were bound to catch up
> with you, and few dogs had ever played dodge-the-car without losing
> on their last turn. But that was the beauty of this particular game. The
> moment you lost, you won. (185–6)

There is no victorious escape from human rule for Mr Bones, only the loss
of his own life. Rather than dealing in polemical critiques of dog slavery or
fantasies of escape, *Timbuktu* instead carefully details two very different ways –
through Willy and Dick – of responding to a relationship that is always already
hierarchical. Encounters and entanglements between humans and dogs,
Auster shows us, are asymmetrical, but this asymmetry can be recognised as
something that shakes the human out of its complacent worldview or it can
be ignored and allow human-centred worldviews to dominate. In reading
Auster's novel the urgent issue facing us is not an abstract and universal moral
question about whether it is cruel to own a pet or not, but rather a concrete,

everyday question of how we think about and treat those animals and how we engage with/in their worlds.

KEY TEXTS

Auster, Paul (1999), *Timbuktu*, London: Faber and Faber.

Derrida, Jacques (2008), *The Animal That Therefore I Am*, trans. David Wills, New York: Fordham University Press.

Derrida, Jacques (2009), *The Beast and the Sovereign*, vol. 1, trans. Geoffrey Bennington, Chicago: University of Chicago Press.

Derrida, Jacques (2011), *The Beast and the Sovereign*, vol. 2, trans. Geoffrey Bennington, Chicago: University of Chicago Press.

Haraway, Donna (2003), *The Companion Species Manifesto: Dogs, People, and Significant Otherness*, Chicago: Prickly Paradigm Press.

Haraway, Donna (2008), *When Species Meet*, Minneapolis: University of Minnesota Press.

Heidegger, Martin (1995), *The Fundamental Concepts of Metaphysics: World, Finitude, Solitude*, trans. William McNeill and Nicholas Walker, Bloomington and Indianapolis: Indiana University Press.

Merleau-Ponty, Maurice (1968), *The Visible and the Invisible*, trans. Alphonso Lingis, Evanston: Northwestern University Press.

Merleau-Ponty, Maurice (2003), *Nature: Course Notes from the Collège de France*, trans. Robert Vallier, Evanston: Northwestern University Press.

Merleau-Ponty, Maurice (2008), *The World of Perception*, trans. Oliver Davis, New York: Routledge.

Montaigne, Michel de (1958), 'Apology for Raymond Sebond', in *The Complete Works of Montaigne: Essays, Travel Journal, Letters*, trans. Donald M. Frame, London: Hamish Hamilton, pp. 318–457.

Uexküll, Jakob von (2010), *A Foray into the Worlds of Animals and Humans with A Theory of Meaning*, trans. Joseph D. O'Neil, Minneapolis: University of Minnesota Press.

FURTHER READING

Agamben, Giorgio (2004), *The Open: Man and Animal*, trans. Kevin Attell, Stanford: Stanford University Press.

Bailey, Christiane (2011), 'Kinds of Life: On the Phenomenological Basis of the Distinction between "Higher" and "Lower" Animals', *Environmental Philosophy* 8.2, 47–68.

Berger, John (2009), *Why Look at Animals?*, London: Penguin.

Berger, Anne Emmanuelle and Marta Segarra (2011), *Demenageries: Thinking (of) Animals After Derrida*, Amsterdam: Rodopi.

Buchanan, Brett (2008), *Onto-Ethologies: The Animal Environments of Uexküll, Heidegger, Merleau-Ponty, and Deleuze*, Albany: State University of New York Press.

Calarco, Matthew (2008), *Zoographies: The Question of the Animal from Heidegger to Derrida*, New York: Columbia University Press.

Cavalieri, Paola (2009), *The Death of the Animal*, New York: Columbia University Press.

DeMello, Margo (2011), 'The Present and Future of Animal Domestication', in Randy Malamud (ed.), *A Cultural History of Animals in the Modern Age*, New York: Berg, pp. 67–94.

DeMello, Margo (2012), 'The Domestication of Animals', in *Animals and Society: An Introduction to Human-Animal Studies*, New York: Columbia University Press, pp. 84–98.

Derrida, Jacques (1996), 'A Silkworm of One's Own (Points of view stitched on the other veil)', *OLR: Oxford Literary Review* 18.1–2, 3–66.

Derrida, Jacques (2001), *Writing and Difference*, trans. Alan Bass, London: Routledge.

Francione, Gary L. (2000), *Introduction to Animal Rights: Your Child or the Dog*, Philadelphia: Temple University Press.

Franklin, Sarah (2007), *Dolly Mixtures: The Remaking of Genealogy*, Durham NC: Duke University Press.

Fudge, Erica (2002), *Animal*, London: Reaktion.

Fudge, Erica (2007), 'The Dog, the Home and the Human, and the Ancestry of Derrida's Cat', *Oxford Literary Review* 29.1–2, 37–54.

Fudge, Erica (2008), *Pets*, Stocksfield: Acumen.

Hearne, Vicki (1994), *Animal Happiness: A Moving Exploration of Animals and Their Emotions*, New York: Skyhorse Publishing.

Hearne, Vicki (2007), *Adam's Task: Calling Animals by Name*, New York: Skyhorse Publishing.

Husserl, Edmund (1960), *Cartesian Meditations: An Introduction to Phenomenology*, trans. Dorion Cairns, The Hague: Martinus Nijhoff.

Husserl, Edmund (1970), *The Crisis of European Sciences and Transcendental Phenomenology*, trans. D. Carr, Evanston: Northwestern University Press.

Husserl, Edmund (1989), *Ideas Pertaining to a Pure Phenomenology and to a Phenomenological Philosophy, Second Book: Studies in the Phenomenology of Constitution*, trans. Richard Rojcewicz and André Schuwer, Dordrecht: Kluwer Academic Publishers.

Ittner, Jutta (2006), 'Part Spaniel, Part Canine Puzzle: Anthropomorphism in Woolf's *Flush* and Auster's *Timbuktu*', *Mosaic* 39.4, 181–96.

Llewelyn, John (2010), 'Where to Cut: Boucherie and Delikatessen', *Research in Phenomenology* 40:2, 161–87.

McHugh, Susan (2004), *Dog*, London: Reaktion.

McNeill, William (1999), 'Life Beyond the Organism: Animal Being in Heidegger's Freiburg Lectures, 1929–30', in H. Peter Steeves (ed.), *Animal Others: On Ethics, Ontology, and Animal Life*, Albany: State University of New York Press, pp. 197–248.

Mazis, Glen A. (2008), *Humans, Animals, Machines: Blurring Boundaries*, Albany: State University of New York Press.

Oliver, Kelly (2009), 'Sexual Difference, Animal Difference: Derrida's Sexy Silkworm', in *Animal Lessons: How They Teach Us to Be Human*, New York: Columbia University Press, pp. 131–54.

Painter, Corinne and Christian Lotz (eds) (2007), *Phenomenology and the Non-Human Animal: At the Limits of Experience*, Dordrecht: Springer.

Rogers, Katharine M. (2006), *Cat*, London: Reaktion.

Serpell, James A. (2005), 'People in Disguise: Anthropomorphism and the Human-Pet Relationship', in Lorraine Daston and Gregg Mitman (eds), *Thinking with Animals: New Perspectives on Anthropomorphism*, New York: Columbia University Press.

Spiegel, Marjorie (1996), *The Dreaded Comparison: Human and Animal Slavery*, New York: Mirror Books.

Turner, Lynn (ed.) (2013), *The Animal Question in Deconstruction*, Edinburgh: Edinburgh University Press.

Velten, Hannah (2007), *Cow*, London: Reaktion.

Westling, Louise (2014), *The Logos of the Living World: Merleau-Ponty, Animals, and Language*, New York: Fordham University Press.

Wood, Sarah (2013), 'Swans of Life (External Provocations and Autobiographical Flights that Teach us How to Read)', in Lynn Turner (ed.), *The Animal Question in Deconstruction*, Edinburgh: Edinburgh University Press.

Wood, Sarah (2014), *Without Mastery: Reading and Other Forces*, Edinburgh: Edinburgh University Press.

CHAPTER 4

Animal Ethics

ANIMAL USES AND ABUSES

It can be difficult to reconcile the human bond with animal life often evident in relations with pets, discussed in Chapter 3, with the realities of the mass slaughter of animals in factory farms, or to reconcile the widespread interest in visiting zoos, discussed in the Introduction, with the realities of the widespread destruction of animal environments for human use. Simply determining that many humans are *cruel* as an explanation for the exploitation of animals doesn't seem adequate. In *The Animal Side*, the contemporary French philosopher Jean-Christophe Bailly points to a paradox in how we respond to the sight of animals in the countryside and how they are treated in global markets of capitalism:

it is clear that at some point there has been a break in the chain between shepherd and butcher, between milk and blood, and that, in response to the familiarity people often establish with animals, we humans end up offering, by killing them, only disavowal and betrayal.

And yet, when we see ewes, cows, or goats wandering in fields, or even when we go into a barn or a stable, what informs our first impression is not a fantasy of domination or mastery, nor is it an economic phenomenon or a technological stratum: there is always . . . a peaceful possibility – a tranquil surge of the world into itself. As long as animals are granted presence in the landscape, there is still a humming to be heard, a possibility of escape . . . It is only when animals are taken out, or kept out, of the landscape that the equilibrium is shattered and that we shift to a regime that is no longer even one of brutality, but rather a regime of dark times in which what is taken away from animals corresponds to the very eradication of all relations with them and to the destruction of any possibility of experience. (2011: 64–5)

A central challenge for animal theorists is to account for ethical responses to animal life at these 'dark times' when we are witnessing the 'eradication of all relations' with many animals. Animal ethics is not only a question of how we treat those pets and zoo animals we come into contact with, but also one of how we ensure that the lives of animals don't disappear entirely from our consideration at a time when we are most likely to encounter them once they are dead and have been turned into products for consumption.

Can They Suffer?

In a now commonly cited passage from his 1781 *Introduction to the Principles of Morals and Legislation*, the British philosopher and social reformer Jeremy Bentham frames the question of ethical responsibility towards animals as one of suffering:

> The day may come when the rest of the animal creation may acquire those rights which never could have been with-holden from them but by the hand of tyranny. The French have already discovered that the blackness of the skin is no reason why a human being should be abandoned without redress to the caprice of a tormentor. It may one day come to be recognized that the number of legs, the villosity of the skin, or the termination of the *os sacrum* are reasons equally insufficient for abandoning a sensitive being to the same fate. What else is it that should trace the insuperable line? Is it the faculty of reason, or perhaps the faculty of discourse? But a full-grown horse or dog is beyond comparison a more rational, as well as a more conversable animal, than an infant of a day or a week or even a month, old. But suppose they were otherwise, what would it avail? The question is not, Can they *reason*? nor Can they *talk*? but, Can they *suffer*? (1982: 283)

Rather than forming a central argument in his book, this passage is actually located in a footnote about the ways in which animals have been 'degraded into the class of things' since the 'ancient jurists'. Nonetheless, it has become significant because Bentham here argues that instead of focusing on physiological or cognitive distinctions between animals as determining our treatment of them, we should consider whether they have a capacity for suffering and, by extension, well-being. The capacity for suffering becomes a foundational consideration of a just response to life. It is important to note that this is not exactly the same as a discourse of 'animal rights', which we will turn to in the following section. Bentham does use the term 'rights' in the above passage, but, as the contemporary moral philosopher Peter Singer reminds us, Bentham's concern is with equal consideration – based on the shared capacity for suffering of humans and animals – rather than asserting prescriptive and universal rights (Singer 1995: 8).

Bentham was a key founder of modern utilitarianism, which broadly argues that moral actions should be based on calculations that maximise benefits to people and limit negative consequences, and Singer's work has, over the past forty years, re-worked this approach to ethics as a way to widely address the mistreatment of animals. Since the publication of his landmark book *Animal Liberation* in 1975, Singer has aimed to challenge the 'tyranny of human over nonhuman animals', a tyranny that is 'as important as any of the moral or social issues that have been fought over in recent years' (1995: ix). The project of liberating nonhuman animals is especially fraught because it requires an act of liberation granted by one species for the benefit of many others; or, put differently, the organising of social protest has to come from the domineering species, rather than from the victims – this makes it distinct from movements for black, women's and gay liberation (xiii). Singer's ethical approach to animals attempts to avoid 'speciesism', a term originally coined by activist Richard Ryder (1971: 81) and in use among a range of posthumanist animal theorists today, as detailed in Chapter 2. Echoing analogous terms like racism and (hetero)sexism, speciesism describes 'a prejudice or attitude of bias in favour of the interests of members of one's own species against those of members of another species' (Singer 1995: 6). It therefore provides a useful term to highlight the long history of human exploitation of animals, and especially the growing abuses of animal life in late capitalism.

The issue of *equality* is central to Singer's project, but it shouldn't be mistaken for a flattening of differences so that every being is reduced to homogeneity or is treated in the same manner: 'The basic principle of equality does not require equal or identical *treatment*; it requires equal consideration. Equal consideration for different beings may lead to different treatments and different rights' (2). This subtle shift from equal treatment to equal consideration results in equality becoming 'a moral idea' rather than an 'assertion of fact' (4). As Singer has re-stated in his introduction to *In Defense of Animals: The Second Wave*, the fight against speciesism 'does not require us to say that all lives are of equal worth, or that all interests of humans and animals must be given equal weight', but it does make

the more limited and defensible claim that where animals and humans have similar interests – we might take the interest in avoiding physical pain as an example – those interests are to be counted equally. We must not disregard or discount the interests of another being, merely because that being is not human. (2006: 7)

Utilitarian thinkers like Singer believe that ethical calculations should be made in an effort to maximise pleasure and minimise pain: whether we are dealing with animals or humans doesn't by itself necessitate any priority over different forms of life because the interests of all are taken into account.

Throughout his work Singer presents many scenarios in which to think through and demonstrate his anti-speciesist ethical position. The following is one example of the 'practical consequences' that follow from his view that it is unjustifiable to give less consideration to the pain or pleasure of a nonhuman animal than that of a human:

> If I give a horse a hard slap across its rump with my open hand, the
> horse may start, but it presumably feels little pain. Its skin is thick
> enough to protect it against a mere slap. If I slap a baby in the same
> way, however, the baby will cry and presumably feel pain, for its skin is
> more sensitive. So it is worse to slap a baby than a horse, if both slaps
> are administered with equal force. But there must be some kind of
> blow – I don't know exactly what it would be, but perhaps a blow with
> a heavy stick – that would cause the horse as much pain as we cause
> a baby by slapping it with our hand . . . and if we consider it wrong
> to inflict that much pain on a baby for no good reason then we must,
> unless we are speciesists, consider it equally wrong to inflict the same
> amount of pain on a horse for no good reason. (1995: 15)

We can see here that the interests of human and nonhuman animals to avoid pain are worthy of consideration. This doesn't mean that the pain suffered by horse and infant in each instance will be identical, but that the logical consequence of the view that it is unethical to cause pain to an infant human should extend to our view of pain experienced by animals.

The four key aspects of utilitarianism are evident in Singer's example: firstly, it is 'universalist' in that the interests of all beings are taken into account; secondly, it is 'welfarist' in that the welfare – the satisfaction of interests – of human and nonhuman animals are of primary concern; thirdly, it is 'consequentialist' in that judgement of whether an action is right or wrong is made by focusing on that action's consequences; and fourthly, it is 'aggregative' because it calculates all interests by adding the interests of those involved and the most ethical action is the one that benefits the greatest number (Matheny 2006: 14–15). In combining these four features the utilitarian approach to animal ethics has advantages in the aim of toppling the historically assumed priority for human concerns. It bases ethical judgements on current knowledge about the world as well as allowing some flexibility in ensuring each scenario that demands an ethical decision is taken on its own terms in relation to all the interested parties. But this approach presents certain problems, too. For an ethics that wants to challenge anthropocentrism, it relies rather heavily on a rationalist, self-aware method of judging the consequences of actions. The emphasis on weighing and measuring places faith in a quantitative calculation that leaves little room for qualitative differences in actions and consequences, and for scenarios which cannot necessarily be reduced to the parts of their sum. That is to say, this approach can feel somewhat abstracted from the messy realities of decision-making, action and consequence, which don't always follow a logical path. Additionally, in utilitarianism humans are of course the ones who make the calculations about interests, pain and suffering. In *Anthropocentrism and Its Discontents*, Gary Steiner suggests that this creates a profound limitation because 'when humans make utilitarian calculations on behalf of animals, the likelihood of anthropocentrism is high' (2005: 9).

Animal Rights

Singer's utilitarian approach has undoubtedly done much to advance debates around animal welfare, and to put animal ethics on the agenda in contemporary moral philosophy. Singer would argue that the benefits of halting the exploitation of animals in factory farms and laboratories as well as the destruction of wild habitats are more significant than any limitations this approach may have. Yet utilitarianism is not the only approach to claim a part in this ethical project, and serious issues have been raised about its theoretical underpinnings that cannot easily be brushed aside. A fundamental challenge to the utilitarian approach has come in the shape of animal rights theory. Tom Regan, in his groundbreaking 1983 study *The Case for Animal Rights*, illustrates that one of the biggest difficulties with utilitarianism is that it views 'use' in human terms and reduces all beings to mere instruments. The focus is on 'the best total balance of good over bad' consequences of actions of everyone, but this could result in allowing a few individuals to 'suffer a lot so that the rest might individually gain a little, the aggregated gain by the many more than compensating for the grievous losses of the few' (1983: 211). In other words, by focusing on quantitative levels of suffering and pleasure, the approach loses sight of the qualitative differences between various human and nonhuman subjects. And so, Regan writes, 'there is no necessary connection, no pre-established harmony between everybody's abiding by the equality principle and everybody's having their interests forwarded equally' (226). The problem with utilitarianism is that beings are not valued *in themselves*. As long as more people benefit from an action than lose out, an action can be justified even if this leads to negative consequences for those in minority groupings.

The limitations of a utilitarian approach are foregrounded, according to Regan, if we consider the example of killing. For the first type of 'hedonistic' utilitarians, associated with Bentham, 'pleasure alone is intrinsically good' and 'pain alone is intrinsically evil' and so moral agents are reduced to 'mere receptacles' of what has this positive and negative value – killing is not in itself judged as unethical (200). Although the second type of 'preference' utilitarianism, associated with Singer, is more complicated and nuanced by the recognition that 'some individuals not only prefer things here and now, they also have preferences regarding their future, in particular *a preference to go on living*', it still creates problems:

> By making this desire [the preference to go on living] a necessary
> condition Singer fails to account for why we have a direct prima facie
> duty not to harm, by killing, animals and those human moral patients
> like these animals in the relevant respects. To desire to continue to live
> presupposes that one have a conception of one's own mortality – that
> one can foresee or anticipate one's eventual demise. And it presupposes,
> further, that, having considered what one's death involves together
> with one's anticipated life prospects, one desires to continue to live in
> preference to dying. It is extremely doubtful that the moral patients at
> issue have the intellectual wherewithal to conceive of their own death
> or to make the kind of comparative judgement Singer's view requires.
> (206)

By following Singer's calculations, certain lives could be valued more than others, leaving some human and nonhuman animals vulnerable to a kind of justified killing. As Regan stresses, 'reliance on the principle of utility could sanction acting in ways where some individuals have their interests affected in significantly adverse ways – for example, they are killed because this brings about optimal aggregated results' (226).

Contrary to the utilitarian approach, Regan argues for 'animal rights'. A now familiar term in western societies, animal rights theorists and activists posit universally recognised principles that take into account the value of each animal's life *in itself*. This view moves from the impersonal, statistical calculations of utilitarianism to an individualist conception of ethics. That is, it doesn't matter if only a few beings are harmed by an action, since those beings have as much right not to be harmed as anyone else. To grant animals 'rights' is to recognise that

> like us, animals have certain basic moral rights, including in particular
> the fundamental right to be treated with the respect that, as possessors
> of inherent value, they are due as a matter of strict justice. Like us,
> therefore . . . they must never be treated as mere receptacles of intrinsic
> values . . . and any harm that is done to them must be consistent with

the recognition of their equal inherent value and their equal prima facie right not to be harmed. (329)

In the rights approach to animal ethics the individual is of 'central importance' (395) in the construction of a list of universal rules or principles, seen for example in Regan's emphasis that *the rights view will not be satisfied with anything less than the total dissolution of the animal industry as we know it*. Firm in the belief that 'all animals are equal, both the plentiful and the rare' (395), Regan's approach refuses to set up hierarchies between species let alone between humans and all other animals.

Granting rights to animals offers a level of protection, in theory and in practice, against their exploitation. While such a project requires political change – brought about by 'those who write letters, circulate petitions, demonstrate, lobby, disrupt a fox hunt, refuse to dissect an animal or to use one in "practice surgery," or are active in other ways' – moral philosophy plays an important role in rigorously putting the question of the ethical status of animals firmly on the agenda in the wider effort to spark 'a revolution in our culture's thought and action' (399–400). Paola Cavalieri's character Alexandra, who in *The Death of the Animal* argues the case for animal rights, suggests that 'in its best philosophical foundation, human rights theory . . . achieves both the reweaving of the connection between intrinsic value and subjectivity and the development of a radically egalitarian framework' (2009: 39). Rather than relying on calculations of consequences, rights offer a way to define clearly what a subject is, what subjects can expect in terms of just treatment, and how their equality is written into law. But much debate has taken place over how far human rights should be extended to animals. Cavalieri's Alexandra defines the criteria for who should qualify for rights as 'simply the fact of being an agent, that is, an intentional being that has goals and wants to achieve them'. This may mean that 'rationality', 'self-consciousness' and 'conceptual-linguistic abilities' are not required, but it still leaves open questions of intentionality, goal-oriented behaviour and want or desire (39). In *The Animal Question*, Cavalieri acknowledges that which 'nonhuman animals meet the requisites for inclusion in the privileged area of full moral status is a problem that cannot yet be settled in detail', but argues that 'among the beings that an *expanded theory of human rights* should cover there undoubtedly are mammals and birds, and probably vertebrates in general' (2001: 139). Herein lies a fundamental problem with the rights approach: it extends a humanist moral framework and humanist conceptions of subjectivity and agency, and so the debate becomes one as to the relevant threshold at which nonhumans qualify to be treated like humans. Cavalieri's chosen subtitle, *Why Nonhuman Animals Deserve Human Rights*, betrays this difficulty; animals are granted entry into human thoughts, but that doesn't necessarily challenge the humanist foundations of this mode of thinking.

Capabilities and Flourishing

A further strand of thought on animal rights has developed out of Martha Nussbaum's 'capabilities' theory, which she describes as 'closely allied to', and even a 'species of', the rights project. In *Frontiers of Justice* she attempts to provide 'precision' and 'supplementation to the language of rights' (2007: 284). Turning to the issue of *flourishing*, the capabilities approach is 'capable of recognizing a wide range of types of animal dignity, and of corresponding needs for flourishing . . . it is attentive to the variety of activities and goals that creatures of many types pursue' (327). The recognition of animal subjectivity is crucial, as with other rights-based approaches, but Nussbaum's concern here isn't only with the basic rights afforded to nonhuman creatures. She opens up a range of (mis)treatments of animals that go beyond the issue of physical cruelty, and in the process mixes rights discourse with a genuine interest in nonhuman modes of life. By considering a range of capabilities that add to 'dignified existence' for all beings, humans and animals alike (326), the capabilities approach is, at its core, about 'a basic wonder at living beings' and 'for a world in which creatures of many types flourish . . . it takes an interest not just in pleasure and pain, but in complex forms of life and functioning. It wants to see each thing flourish as the sort of thing it is' (349). Nussbaum wants to account more precisely and practically for what helps and hinders an animal in its efforts to fulfil its distinct potential. She attempts, therefore, to find more nuanced reasons *why* various practices are, or are not, ethical.

Frontiers of Justice lists numerous items that the capabilities approach seeks to measure flourishing by. This includes the basic entitlement to 'Life', but also a range of other entitlements in terms of 'Bodily Health' and 'Bodily Integrity', as well as the flourishing of senses, imagination, thought, emotions, play and a capability to control one's environment among other things. We can think back here to the kinds of questions posed by Derrida in Chapter 3 about animal capacities that philosophers have previously failed to consider and say that Nussbaum wants to engage with the realities of such capacities. With all of these capabilities there is an ongoing discussion about what leads to flourishing and what doesn't, and it is not simply a case of equalising the entitlements of all animals (or of human and animal, or even of all creatures within a particular species) within each capability. To see this we can consider two of the items listed: 'Life' and 'Bodily Integrity'. Firstly, with the question of life, 'all animals are entitled to continue their lives, whether or not they have such a conscious interest, unless and until pain and decrepitude make death no longer a harm'. But the decision about this is different for humans and animals, as well as for different animals: 'This entitlement is less robust when we are dealing with insects and other nonsentient or minimally sentient forms of life'

(393). Already we find three categories of creatures: the sentient, the nonsentient, and the minimally sentient.

Secondly, we can consider the example of 'Bodily Integrity', the entitlement to avoid manipulations and mutilations of the body: 'animals have direct entitlements against violations of their bodily integrity by violence, abuse, and other forms of harmful treatment – whether or not the treatment in question is painful'. Here there is clearly an advantage over approaches that focus primarily on suffering, but potential difficulties arise in some other examples Nussbaum turns to. Consider her view on the role of training, which involves disciplining animal bodies. For Nussbaum, 'the fact that a horse is at first annoyed by the bridle is not a negative thing in the capabilities approach, any more than is the annoyance of human children at compulsory schooling' – the latter is 'justified', she adds, 'in its role of promoting adult flourishing and capability' (395). This recalls the arguments of Vicki Hearne, who in *Animal Happiness* suggests that horse training is a form of education like teaching children so that their talent is fulfilled (1994: 204). However, such analogies are never as straightforward as they seem. Of course compulsory schooling does, most people agree, enhance capabilities of humans. But there are aspects of compulsory schooling that don't necessarily help children to flourish (we may think of the history of corporal punishment, and various ways in which school children's potential capabilities are hindered by poor resources, by curricula design, or by different styles of teaching). 'Training' and 'schooling' may to some extent be analogous, but there is much scope for debate about the specificities of each. Moreover, we might ask whether training horses only helps them to flourish as the type of horses humans want them to become.

Another related bodily issue is the capability for sexual reproduction and pleasure. Nussbaum is in no doubt this should be granted to humans, but with animals she claims the issue is more complex. While 'it would seem good to protect this capability for animals', notes Nussbaum, 'the castrating of certain male animals (horses, dogs, cats) seems (on the basis of long experience) to be compatible with flourishing lives for those animals'. Such bodily mutilation seems more acceptable for animals because they have 'lesser capacity for character change and choice. One cannot tell a dog inclined to aggression to change and behave differently; so castration may in many cases be the course most appropriate to its own flourishing and that of other animals' (2007: 395–6). Not only does this statement make assumptions about dogs' capacities for change, but when extended to human ethics it raises uncomfortable questions: what would we think if these attitudes were directed towards aggressive humans? Additionally, what would happen if a certain amount of aggression and violence is central to the flourishing of a particular animal? In comparison to Regan, these examples display both an advantage of Nussbaum's approach, namely that it deals with specificities and allows finer scrutiny of these issues, and also a limitation, in that it complicates the process of who deserves what rights to the point where violence against certain animals could be tolerated more than violence against others. A key question that remains is: who decides what it is to flourish?

Nussbaum's capabilities approach is helpful because it provides humans with a practical way of thinking through ethical quandaries. Its emphasis is on gradual change, and it doesn't posit a utopian solution (the kind which can sometimes fail before it begins precisely because of its ambition): 'We should admit', she writes, 'that there will be an ineliminable residue of tragedy in the relationships between humans and animals' (404). But in a sense this is also the biggest drawback of the approach – it simply is not radical enough. Firstly, this can be seen by the fact that Nussbaum extends a theoretical framework that is, at its core, based on the liberal individual subject:

> What we want political actors to do, in a liberal state, is *just* to take care of basic justice, and not to be maximisers of overall good. We actively want them *not* to pursue the maximization of overall good, because we don't want them to be in the business of defining what the good is in a comprehensive way. The right division of labor in a liberal society is for political institutions to take care of justice, and for individuals to be left free to pursue on their own other parts of their comprehensive conceptions of the good. (340)

Nussbaum's theory works within, rather than seeks to challenge, the status quo of neoliberal capitalism, where the state remains small and individuals are supposedly free to flourish on their own terms. Yet, given the number of humans and animals oppressed within this system, it is not at all clear that this version of the individual leads to the best form of flourishing. A second problem is Nussbaum's emphasis on 'species norms', where she writes that 'the species norm (duly evaluated) tells us what the appropriate benchmark is for judging whether a given creature has decent opportunities for flourishing'. We should have 'a commitment to bring members of that species up to that norm' (363–5). This model runs the risk of overlooking exceptions and those who don't fit neatly into normative categories. In 'reasserting classical humanist ideals and progressive liberal politics', Nussbaum's animal ethics complements her wider moral project which is, as Rosi Braidotti argues, 'a thorough contemporary defence of Humanism as the guarantee of democracy, freedom and the respect for human dignity' that fails to seriously engage the idea that humanism is in crisis 'let alone the possibility of its historical decline' (2013: 38). Nussbaum's thinking is therefore at odds with the critiques of humanism among many posthumanist theorists, discussed in Chapter 2, for whom ideological critique is central to attempts to challenge anthropocentrism and speciesism.

BEYOND ANIMAL RIGHTS

As approaches all working within the 'analytic' tradition of philosophy, with its emphasis on conceptual clarity, the three examples of animal ethics above place their faith in rational judgement, logical argumentation and autonomous subjectivity. But many animal theorists aligned with the 'continental' tradition – to which belong the majority of thinkers explored in the previous chapters of this book – have challenged precisely these modes and models of thought. We might wonder how we can base an ethics on rationality, logic and the notion of autonomous subjects without that ethics being anthropocentric. Because of the divergence in methodology between analytic and continental philosophers, one of the challenges for animal theorists is, then, to create greater dialogue between the traditions so that these thinkers, many of whom share similar ethical concerns, might help to inform and critique one another. The potential for conversation across methodological divides available in considerations of the ethical treatment of animals is demonstrated in the aforementioned *The Death of the Animal*, which stages a dialogue between Paola Cavalieri and Harlan Miller, whose work is aligned with analytic philosophy, and Cary Wolfe and Matthew Calarco, who primarily engage with continental thought. As Peter Singer notes in his foreword to the book, it is 'one of the rare occasions in which people coming out of the analytic and the continental traditions actually meet in discussions on a specific subject and connect with each other's positions' (Cavalieri 2009: x). As well as offering a wider exploration of animal ethics, reading analytic and continental philosophy side-by-side also illustrates how engaging with the 'question of the animal' can challenge us to think more about the very way that we think. Following the analytic approaches to ethical animal theory discussed above, this section considers further limitations of their discourse through critiques from within both the analytic and continental traditions.

Fellow Creatures

In her 1978 article 'Eating Meat and Eating People', analytic philosopher Cora Diamond outlines limitations with animal rights views in terms of what she calls 'fundamental confusions about moral relations between people and people *and* between people and animals'. Responding to Singer's critique of speciesism in *Animal Liberation*, and to the growing considerations of the interests of animals in ethical theory that emerged around the time that Singer's book was published, Diamond claims that the analogies drawn between human actions towards humans and human actions towards animals are much too simplistic. She takes issue with the ways in which an approach based on universal, rational and *quantitative* calculations of suffering 'makes it hard to see what is important *either* in our relationships with other human beings *or* in our relationship with animals' (1978: 467). Such ethical models don't tell us enough about the *qualitative* aspects of human-animal relations.

To illustrate her central concern with the limitations of anti-speciesist approaches to ethics, Diamond turns to the issue of eating animals. The problem with utilitarian and rights-based theories is that they depend on quantitative comparisons of interests and suffering that mistakenly assume that vegetarians don't eat animals because killing animals would cause too much pain (and that this is the same reason humans don't kill other humans to eat them). But focusing on a threshold of suffering as the benchmark of what our ethical treatment of animals should attend to misses the point about the reason many vegetarians don't eat animals, which shares something with the real reason humans don't eat other humans. That is, we cannot say that quantities of suffering alone stop us from eating humans, because most humans wouldn't want to eat another human even if there was no evidence that anyone would suffer directly or indirectly from doing so (for example, if the human had already died of natural causes and had no relatives). Diamond's argument is that we should realise vegetarians often don't eat animals for the same qualitative reason that they don't eat humans – namely, that animals are simply not *there* to be eaten: 'There is nothing in the discussion which suggests that a cow is *not* something to eat; it is only that one must not help the process along: one must not, that is, interfere with those rights that we should usually have to interfere with if we are to eat animals at all conveniently' (468). The emphasis on numbers of dead or quantities of suffering fails to account for the view that we shouldn't eat animals simply because we share life with them – the same reason we don't eat other humans. Levels of suffering may be part of the reason for not eating animals but this doesn't sufficiently account for the deeper ontological and ethical point.

We will return to the issue of eating animals later in this chapter, but we can broaden out Diamond's focus on our qualitative relationship with animals to other ethical issues. In place of discussion about capacities and rights, Diamond urges that we think of 'fellow creatures' as the 'direction in which [we] should look for an answer'. Crucially, this view of fellow creatures depends on distinctly human *experiences* rather than being a category that is determined by biological features. In the writings of utilitarians and rights theorists she finds problematic the way that the argument starts

> supposedly from the biological fact that we and dogs and rats and titmice and monkeys are all species of animal, differentiated indeed in terms of this or the other capacity, but what is appropriate treatment for members of our species would be appropriate to members of any whose capacities gave them similar interests. We are all equally animals,

though, for a start – with, therefore, an equal right to have whatever our interests are taken into account. The starting point for our thought is what is general and in common and biologically given. (474)

For Diamond, fellowship doesn't suggest belonging to the same biological category but instead indicates a kind of cultural attitude or behaviour. Her preferred notion of a 'fellow creature' is presented as that 'which is *not* a biological concept. It doesn't mean, biologically an animal, something with *biological life.*' Rather, it means 'fellows in mortality, in life on this earth' and this 'depends upon a conception of *human* life. It is an extension of a non-biological notion of what human life is.' It is, in other words, precisely by being human that we have fellowship with animals. If we empty humans of all distinct humanity, then we fail to recognise that the 'moral expectations of other human beings demand something of me as other than an animal'. Diamond argues, then, that it is disingenuous to destroy the distinction between humans and animals when making ethical calculations while only holding one species – the human – to the resulting moral standard: we cannot define a specifically human ethical response and at the same time 'destroy its foundation' (478). On the contrary, for Diamond, as Cary Wolfe notes, 'it is not by denying the special status of "human being" but rather, as it were, by intensifying it that we can come to think of nonhuman animals not as bearers of "interests" or as "rights holders" but rather as something much more compelling' (2008: 15).

In terms of the practical benefits of this more compelling emphasis on 'fellow creatures', Diamond notes that some people will never be capable of extending such fellowship to animals – her approach 'is not usable with someone in whom there is no fellow-creature response, nothing at all in that range'. But this practical limitation is particularly relevant where utilitarianism and animal rights theory is concerned, because the idea of fellowship is concrete whereas universal animal rights is 'an abstract principle of equality' (1978: 477). In other words, those who base their ethics on universal rights can never speak for everyone and everything, and in claiming they can they fail to provide precise enough ways of thinking about ethics that would take into account a wide variety of humans living in different contexts and with different capacities for imagination or sympathy. While we often speak as though hard facts – quantifiable numbers and statistics – are concrete indicators of reality, Diamond's essay reminds us that that which is qualitative, and therefore difficult to neatly categorise, is actually most concrete of all. However hard it is to come by fellowship, however elusive it may be, it is much better to try to work through difficult qualitative questions about what it means for humans to mistreat animals than resort to the shortcut of abstract calculations or principles. Utilitarianism and the varieties of rights-based theories fail to acknowledge, account for and respond to animals *as* animals and injustice *as* injustice.

Unrecognisable Ethics

In continental philosophy, Derrida has stated his sympathy with animal rights, even if he doesn't offer a clear practical outline of how animals should and shouldn't be treated in the way that some rights theorists do. While in 'strong sympathy' with the Universal Declaration of Animal Rights (Derrida 2008: 88), he does, however, raise fundamental questions about what the idea of a 'right' means, what assumptions about subjectivity these rights are based on, and how successful animal rights can be if they are simply integrated into existing legal frameworks which are founded on humanist, anthropocentric viewpoints. As he puts it in his interview with Elizabeth Roudinesco on 'Violence Against Animals':

> to want absolutely to grant, not to animals but to a certain category
> of animals, rights equivalent to human rights would be a disastrous
> contradiction. It would reproduce the philosophical and juridical
> machine thanks to which the exploitation of animal material for food,
> work, experimentation . . . has been practiced (and tyrannically so, that
> is, through an abuse of power).

Derrida dismisses faith in 'the miracle of legislation' as the sole vehicle for change in relations between humans and animals (2004: 65). Elsewhere he writes of animal rights as too 'dependent on a philosophy of the subject of a Cartesian or Kantian type, which is the very philosophy in the name of which the animal is reduced to the status of a machine without reason and without personhood'. Animal rights theory is therefore 'a major failure of logic' (2009: 111). Rather that theorising which rights should and shouldn't be granted to animals, the real question becomes: rights on whose terms?

In *The Beast and the Sovereign*, Derrida presents an alternative to an ethics based on 'rights'. He considers a principle of 'justice' that is founded on 'responsibility with respect to the most dissimilar . . . the entirely other . . . the unrecognizable other'. In recognising, and crucially *responding* to, the alterity of the unrecognisable, Derrida seeks to uproot the bias in an ethics extended to animals from human rights:

> The 'unrecognizable' . . . is the beginning of ethics, of the Law, and
> not of the human. So long as there is recognizability and fellow, ethics
> is dormant. It is sleeping a dogmatic slumber. So long as it remains
> human, among men, ethics remains dogmatic, narcissistic, and not yet
> thinking . . . The 'unrecognizable' is the awakening. It is what awakens,
> the very experience of being awake. (2009: 108)

Here Derrida resists the simple incorporation of animals into a human moral code. Unlike the three approaches outlined in the first part of this chapter, it is not enough to simply build on or extend an ethics based on humanist models which either calculate suffering (utilitarianism), construct universal principles (rights), or cultivate dignified modes of life (capabilities). Instead, if we are to provide an ethics that is truly open to nonhuman as well as human 'others', we must probe the existing anthropocentric frameworks through which we think of ethics. It is only this that has the potential to truly transform the relationship between 'humans' and 'animals' because it depends on a transformation of how we conceptualise both these categorisations.

Derrida's wider approach to animality, outlined in Chapter 3, can, as Wolfe has pointed out, appear similar to Diamond's in three ways: firstly, the emphasis on shared vulnerability and finitude; secondly, the idea that ethics is an ongoing process that is never settled; and thirdly, the fundamental role that language plays in blinding us to the realities of both of these first two aspects (Wolfe 2008: 16–19). But responding to that which we cannot necessarily recognise means that we have to think beyond Diamond's conceptualisation of others as 'fellow creatures' – indeed *The Beast and the Sovereign* defines the unrecognisable as 'the non-fellow' (2009: 108). Derrida therefore seeks to move on from all the ways in which we might base our ethics on fellowship, including family, nation, race, culture and religion:

> If one trusts and binds oneself to a Law that refers us only to the similar, the fellow . . . that means, correlatively, that one has obligations only to the fellow, be it the foreigner as fellow and 'my neighbour,' which, step by step, as we know, in fact intensifies our obligations toward the most similar and the nearest . . . More obligation toward men than toward animals, more obligation toward men who are close and similar than toward the less close and less similar (in the order of probabilities and supposed or fantasized resemblances or similarities: family, nation, race, culture, religion). One will say that this is a *fact* (but can a fact ground and justify an ethics?): it is a fact that I feel, in this order, more obligations toward those who closely share my life, my people, my family, the French, the Europeans, those who speak my language or share my culture . . . But this fact will never have founded a right, an ethics, or a politics. (108–9)

Evident here is Derrida's profoundly anti-parochial consideration of animals that uproots ethics from 'fact', from what appears familiar and naturally true. It is this more radical critique that marks the divide between Derrida's 'post-humanism' and Diamond's 'humanism', and that also marks a divide between the continental and analytic approaches to animal theory (Wolfe 2010: 89–90).

Derrida's animal ethics is, to some extent, indebted to another continental philosopher, Emmanuel Levinas, and specifically his view of ethics as 'first philosophy'. For Levinas ethics comes before being, it is 'the laying down by the ego of its sovereignty' in the 'face of the other'. Disrupting the understanding of ethics as a rational process, it becomes a matter of opening oneself up to an encounter with otherness by putting otherness *before* oneself. Thus Levinas theorises an ethical response to radical alterity that is *not* an incorporation of the 'other' into the 'same' (or the self) (1989: 84–5). But the limitation of Levinas' originary ethics for Derrida is that the animal fails to fully qualify as an ethical 'other' because it is deprived of language. When asked in an interview if the animal has a '"face" in the ethical sense' Levinas equivocates: 'I cannot say at what moment you have the right to be called "face." The human face is completely different and only afterwards do we discover the face of an animal. I don't know if a snake has a face. I can't answer that question. A more specific analysis is needed' (1988: 171–2). In contrast to this, Derrida seeks an ethical response to animals that doesn't depend upon language or recognition. He deconstructs Levinas' anthropocentric ethics of the 'face', where the animal is 'outside of the ethical circuit' (Derrida 2008: 106). Levinas' 'nonresponse' to the question of whether the animal, and specifically the snake here, has a face is 'all too human', illustrating the same bias that has permeated European philosophical discourse from Descartes to Kant to Heidegger (108–9). In turning to the snake with its 'immense allegorical or mythical weight' that typically ties it to evil (110), Levinas enacts a kind of diversion that avoids confronting this difficult question about a multiplicity of animals, a question that threatens to uproot the very foundations of his ethics grounded in the potential for human discourse.

There is, nonetheless, one intriguing occasion where Levinas does explicitly address an animal in his writings. This occurs in a short piece about a dog, Bobby, he encountered when in a Nazi concentration camp. After being made 'subhuman, a gang of apes', by imprisonment, Levinas recalls:

> about halfway through our long captivity, for a few short weeks, before the sentinels chased him away, a wandering dog entered our lives.
> One day he came to meet this rabble as we returned under guard from work. He survived in some wild patch in the region of the camp. But we called him Bobby, an exotic name, as one does with a cherished dog. He would appear at morning assembly and was waiting for us as we returned, jumping up and down and barking in delight. For him, there was no doubt that we were men. (2004: 49)

Here the human-turned-subhuman comes face-to-face with the animal. Levinas appears to ascribe to the dog a power to address and be addressed ethically, and we know from his comments in the aforementioned interview that he is at least open to the possibility of a dog having a 'face' even though the face is found 'in its purest form' in humans rather than canines (1988: 169). Yet, crucially, the encounter very clearly restores the humanity of the human – that 'we were men' – rather than pointing to any affinity in terms of a shared animality. Levinasian ethics may come before being, but it is oriented towards humanity. By contrast, Derrida suggests that animals demand a response even as they are turned away from the human, even as they cannot be recognised as having a 'face' or language. Truly addressing the vast scope of cruelty towards animals requires an unrecognisable ethics that responds to that which cannot speak, that which never faces towards us.

EATING ANIMALS

The most impassioned debates in animal ethics are concerned with those animals we rarely, in twenty-first-century western societies, come face-to-face with in living form; that is, those animals that are killed and eaten in huge numbers on a daily basis. We frequently assume that eating animals is something that humans have always done, yet the concept of vegetarianism has a long history. One of the earliest proponents of a meat-free diet, the ancient Greek philosopher Plutarch, reverses the usual approach to eating animals by stating that we shouldn't ask why people abstain from meat so much as ask why people started to eat meat in the first place:

> I for my part do much wonder in what humor, with what soul or
> reason, the first man with his mouth touched slaughter, and reached to
> his lips the flesh of a dead animal . . . how his sight could endure the
> blood of slaughtered, flayed, and mangled bodies; how his smell could
> bear their scent; and how the very nastiness happened not to offend the
> taste, while it chewed the sores of others, and participated of the saps
> and juices of deadly wounds. (2007: 154–5)

This passage is especially important in returning us to the fleshly realities of where meat comes from. But Plutarch does something further here, too. He exposes the myth of meat eating as *natural* by turning to the human body:

> that it is not natural to mankind to feed on flesh, we first of all
> demonstrate from the very shape and figure of the body. For a human
> body no ways resembles those that were born for ravenousness; it hath

> no hawk's bill, no sharp talon, no roughness of teeth, no such strength
> of stomach or heat of digestion . . . if you will contend that yourself was
> born to an inclination to such food as you have now a mind to eat, do
> you then yourself kill what you would eat. But do it yourself, without
> the help of a chopping-knife, mallet, or axe, – as wolves, bears, and
> lions do, who kill and eat at once . . . Nay, there is nobody that is willing
> to eat even a lifeless and a dead thing as it is; but they boil it, and roast
> it, and alter it by fire and medicines, as it were, changing and quenching
> the slaughtered gore with thousands of sweet sauces. (156)

The way in which we kill, cook and season meat serves to distance it from its animal origins. We naturalise the killing and eating of animals even though this has always been a culturally variable process.

The eighteenth-century philosopher Jean-Jacques Rousseau followed Plutarch in presenting an argument as to the culturally constructed nature of eating animals. *Emile, or On Education* suggests that we only need to look at the types of food children prefer to see that their appetite is not always and already one that needs to be satiated by meat: 'One of the proofs that the taste for meat is not natural to man is the indifference that children have for that kind of food and the preference they all give to vegetable foods, such as dairy products, pastry, fruits, etc. It is, above all, important not to denature this primitive taste and make children carnivorous.' The natural attitude of humans towards meat is here claimed to be one of indifference; it is only cultural expectations that lead to the widespread appetite for meat. For Rousseau, the violence inherent in the process of meat eating is of concern to human health but also 'character':

> however one explains the experience, it is certain that great eaters of
> meat are in general more cruel and ferocious than other men. This is
> observed in all places and all times. English barbarism is known . . . All
> savages are cruel, and it is not their morals which cause them to be so.
> This cruelty comes from their food. They go to war as to the hunt and
> treat men like bears . . . Great villains harden themselves to murder by
> drinking blood. (1979: 153)

In being linked to a violent masculinity, meat eating is conceived as a threat *to* human cultures, created *by* human cultures.

The fleshly realities of where meat comes from, and the de-naturalisation of the carnivorous diet, has never been more relevant than in today's context, where animals are systematically slaughtered by humans in greater numbers than has ever been done before by any other species. We have moved from times when meat was eaten very rarely, to meat being sought through hunting, to meat from domesticated animals kept to provide food, to the post-industrial, late capitalist model of factory farms (Adams 2010: 91). Meat eating has never been more popular, where upwards of 50 billion animals are estimated to be killed each year for consumption, which is a fivefold increase since 1950 (Gruen 2011: 81). Nor has eating animals ever been more culturally mediated, to the point where advertising and packaging for supermarkets conceals any sign of the brutality in how the meat is produced. As the historian Chris Otter puts it: 'That rows of wrapped, severed cubes of flesh, perhaps adorned with labels decorated with cartoon pigs or cows, are *just there* in the shop, next to smiling children and sweet old men, is one of the strangest normal things in our world' (2008: 106). It is against the backdrop of this 'strangest normal' phenomenon that contemporary animal theorists approach the ethical issue of eating animals.

The Sexual Politics of Meat

While Rousseau's concern is primarily for eighteenth-century morality, the turn to issues of eating animals among activists and scholars in more recent years has similarly attempted to de-naturalise the process of meat eating and also tied it to a wider culture of patriarchal violence. One of the most influential and controversial interventions into the theory and practice of eating animals came in 1990 with the publication of Carol Adams' *The Sexual Politics of Meat: A Feminist Vegetarian Critical Theory*. Engaging with a range of cultural representations, this study draws analogies between meat eating and the oppression of women. As Adams writes in the preface to the twentieth anniversary edition of the book, the sexual politics of meat is 'an attitude and action that animalizes women and sexualizes and feminizes animals' (2010: 4). Patriarchy, Adams argues, creates the expectation that power and virility should be expressed by men through misogynistic attitudes and behaviours towards women as well as through the eating of meat; as victims of this power dynamic women and animals share oppressed identities. In being judged as lacking rationality women have historically been aligned with animals, and as Adams and Josephine Donovan comment in the later *Animals and Women*, there are three main ways feminists have responded to this: by arguing, as Simone de Beauvoir does in *The Second Sex*, that women are not like animals and should aim for transcendence to put them on a level with man; to work with this connection between women and animals to expose their shared oppression; or finally to claim that feminism has nothing to do with animals and in fact that focusing on animals only distracts from far more important issues facing women (Adams and Donovan 1995: 1–3). It is in the second of these historical trends that we can position Adams' work.

Central to this theory of the interrelationship between women's and animals' oppression is what Adams calls the 'absent referent', which describes a phenomenon whereby patriarchal cultural practices obscure the embodied realities of women and animals. Where meat is concerned, Adams points to three ways in which actual animals are made invisible, all of which have equivalents in violence against women. First is a quite literal rendering of absence, where 'through meat eating they are literally absent because they are dead'. Here we can think about how neatly diced or minced pieces of meat appear on dinner plates and how this, in the process, encourages humans to disassociate the food product from the animals who are killed. The second manner of animals becoming absent referents is 'definitional: when we eat animals we change the way we talk about them' (Adams 2010: 66). We might think here about how, in the English language at least, the names we provide for animals that are alive, and those on the table, are different: 'After being butchered fragmented body parts are often renamed to obscure the fact that these were once animals.' Once they are dead, cows are transformed into 'roast beef, steak, hamburger' and pigs into 'pork, bacon, sausage'. 'We opt', Adams adds, 'for less disquieting referent points' in the way we name meat but also in how we cook and season these meaty objects, therefore 'disguising their original nature', to echo Plutarch's argument (74). Finally, the third way in which animals become absent referents is through figurative language such as when they 'become metaphors for describing people's experiences' so that 'the meaning of the absent referent derives from its application or reference to something else' (67). Here we might think about the figurative use of the word 'meat' to describe the 'meat of the matter' or 'a meaty question', meaning something substantial. A phrase like 'beef up' means that something needs to become stronger, or be improved, and we can compare this with the word 'vegetable' which has the opposite connotations. As a metaphor, 'Meat is *something one enjoys or excels in*, vegetable becomes representative of someone who does not enjoy anything: a *person who leads a monotonous, passive, or merely physical existence*' (60). Taken together, these three deep-rooted, interrelated processes outlined by Adams render absent the animal *as* animal in the eating of meat.

Adams foregrounds a range of examples of how the cultural practice of meat eating reinforces 'patriarchal values' and can be linked to the subjugation of women (67). This manifests itself in the ways in which, both materially and figuratively, men who are violent towards women are also frequently violent towards animals. For example, Adams points to a range of cases of sexual abuse and murder where animals have been used for intimidation or have themselves been killed and outlines how in pornography and prostitution the language used to describe women evokes the slaughter and consumption of animals (71; 68). Additionally, the very ways in which women's body parts are objectified is itself a form of 'butchering' and the pervasiveness of this attitude is seen in advertising, film and literature (86–7). Such instances can be understood through 'a paradigm of metaphorical sexual butchering' which consists of: a real or metaphorical 'knife' (for pornography read 'camera lens'); an 'aggressor' who wants to 'control/consume/defile the body of the victim'; and the 'fetishism of body parts'. What is crucial to note is that the association of women's bodies with meat is always part of an objectifying process. The challenge for feminists is not only to critique and liberate women from being 'treated like pieces of meat – emotionally butchered and physically battered', but also to recognise and respond to the ways in which 'animals actually are made into pieces of meat' (72).

In a sense what Adams is attempting to challenge is what Derrida, in his very different style of theorising, has termed 'carno-phallogocentrism'. With this term he points to the ways in which subjectivity is often reserved not only for humans, but for meat-eating men. In his interview with fellow French philosopher Jean-Luc Nancy, '"Eating Well," or the Calculation of the Subject', Derrida explains how the dominant 'schema' of subjectivity 'implies carnivorous virility'; it denotes a 'virile figure at the determinative center of the subject' (1991: 113–14). This metaphysical exclusion of subjectivity is linked to a wider range of oppressed or minority identities:

Authority and autonomy (for even if autonomy is subject to the law, this subjugation is freedom) are, through this schema, attributed to man (*homo* and *vir*) rather than to woman, and to the woman rather than to the animal. And of course to the adult rather than to the child. The virile strength of the adult male, the father, husband, or brother . . . belongs to the schema that dominates the concept of subject. (114)

This adult male authority and autonomy depends upon the eating of flesh, a point that Derrida emphasises by rhetorically asking how possible it would be to envisage a western head of state gaining power if s/he identified as vegetarian and supported vegetarianism: 'in our countries, who would stand any chance of becoming a *chef d'État* . . . by publicly, and therefore exemplarily, declaring him- or herself to be a vegetarian?' He goes on to conclude that 'the *chef* must be an eater of flesh . . . to say nothing of the celibate, of homosexuality, and even', he adds, 'of femininity (which for the moment, and so rarely, is only admitted to the head of whatever it might be, especially the State, if it lets itself be translated into a virile and heroic schema' (114). Derrida therefore links a range of groups, and especially women, who are discriminated against so as to draw connections between the absence of vegetarianism and the absence of femininity at the seat of power. Punning on the French 'chef', he stresses that all too often power goes hand-in-hand with meat eating.

One crucial difference between Adams and Derrida can be located, however, in the way that they link theory to practice. Adams' solution to her project is an 'ethical vegetarianism' that 'regards meat eating as an unjustifiable exploitation of other animals' (2010: 30). It is through this form of vegetarianism that a different worldview also emerges to challenge the patriarchal status quo. Terming it 'the vegetarian quest', Adams outlines three main stages. Firstly, the 'nothingness of meat' is exposed through recognition of the absent referent; in other words, we recognise that meat itself is an animal (227). Secondly, having recognised the animal, an act of *'naming the relationships'* takes place. 'These relationships include: the connection between meat on the table and a living animal; between ourselves and the other animals; between our ethics and our diet; and the recognition of the needless violence of meat eating.' Resultantly, 'the interpretation moves from the nothingness of meat to the conviction that killing animals is wrong' (229). Thirdly, the personal quest takes on a public and more political dimension as *'rebuking a meat-eating world'*, where vegetarianism affirms an alternative to the meat-eating norm. In keeping with its feminist dimension, such a vegetarianism, for Adams, 'rebukes a patriarchal society' as 'meat eating is associated with male power' (231).

There is something seductive about this straightforward plan, which allows Adams' theory of the absent referent to translate neatly onto the personal and political action of ethical vegetarianism. It is difficult to argue that such an approach wouldn't benefit animals, or that it wouldn't challenge certain levers of capitalism (given how many animals are killed each year for meat, and how lucrative the global meat industry is). But what is less clear is how realistic a plan it is, and also how vegetarianism would help with the oppression of women. If women all become vegetarians, it doesn't follow that men will. Indeed, such an event might be counter-productive to women's liberation from patriarchy; if men continue to eat meat and women less so, then it surely would only reinforce the associations between male virility and meat eating. The myth that 'men are strong, men need to be strong, thus men need meat' wouldn't necessarily break down (and may even be strengthened). Moreover, Adams' approach is in danger of itself aligning women with passivity and the very associations she seeks to overcome. Consider a notorious passage from German philosopher G. W. F. Hegel's *Elements of the Philosophy of Right*, first published in 1821, which details how 'the difference between man and woman is the difference between animal and plant; the animal is closer to man, the plant to woman, for the latter is a more peaceful [process of] unfolding whose principle is the more indeterminate unity of feeling' (Hegel 1991: 207). Adams interprets this statement as sending a message, once again, that 'both women and plants are seen as less developed and less evolved than men and animals' with the implication that 'women may eat plants since each is placid; but active men need animal meat' (2010: 61). While women may be associated with animals in a process of objectification, they are never defined as subjects by their eating of animals in the way men are.

In addition, we need to be wary of thinking that feminist vegetarians necessarily have a closer relationship to living animals. Consider the curious remark, made by Luce Irigaray in 'Animal Compassion', that dogs act differently towards her because she no longer eats meat:

> I have noticed something interesting in this regard: the fact that I have become vegetarian, which means for me giving up killing to eat, has made certain animals, dogs, for example, more friendly to me. A silent non-aggressive pact exists between us. Having less fear, they attack less. And I, for my part, experience less fear toward them. (2004: 198)

In claiming that dogs share a 'silent non-aggressive pact' with her, Irigaray suggests that animals across species lines share such a pact and are therefore attuned to the same ethical concerns she has about eating animals. Not only does this seem to be somewhat removed from the various eating habits of different animals, but the implications for feminism are difficult to endorse. It is surely problematic to view women who eat meat as lesser feminists, as is implied by Adams' argument, or as less capable of forming bonds with pet animals, to follow the logic of Irigaray's claim.

Derrida, on the other hand, never advocates vegetarianism as a solution to the shared oppression of women and animals (although he certainly doesn't negate it as a challenge to the carno-phallogocentric structures of thought and society): 'I do not believe', he writes, 'in absolute "vegetarianism," nor in the ethical purity of its intentions – nor even that it is rigorously tenable, without a compromise or without a symbolic substitution.' He goes even further in adding that 'in a more or less refined, subtle, sublime form, a certain cannibalism remains unsurpassable' (2004: 67). Derrida warns, then, that we must be careful to avoid the intimation that by simply becoming vegetarian we can be ethically cleansed of responsibility in the violence against animals. In '"Eating Well"' he argues that

> vegetarians, too, partake of animals, even of men . . . The moral question is thus not, nor has it ever been: should one eat or not eat, eat this and not that, the living or the nonliving, man or animal, but since *one must* eat in any case and since it tastes good to eat, and since there's no other definition of the good (*du bien*), how for goodness sake should one eat well (*bien manger*)? And what does this imply? What is eating? How is this metonymy of introjection to be regulated? And in what

respect does the formulation of these questions in language give us
still more food for thought? In what respect is the question, if you will,
carnivorous? (1991: 115)

In this somewhat cryptic passage Derrida poses a range of questions which are
more difficult to answer than the question of whether one should or shouldn't
eat meat. He attempts to probe what it means to ask such questions in human
language in the first place, drawing attention to the fact that in the act of iden-
tifying, naming and relating to nonhuman life there will always be at least a
symbolic violence towards animals. As Lynn Turner puts it, 'even when we
refuse to eat meat or consume animal products more widely, we nevertheless
"eat meat" through ingestion as identification' (2013: 61). While Derrida is not
claiming that all forms of real or symbolic violence can be equated – though
he has been seen by some critics to 'sidestep' the material realities of cruelty
towards animals (Wood 1999: 31–3) – he is eager to guard against 'compla-
cency' and 'good conscience' by suggesting that 'the ideal of ethical purity is
ruled out a priori as structurally impossible' (Calarco 2008: 136). Derrida's
analysis doesn't entirely forego the important ethical potential of vegetarianism but nor does it reach for it as the solution, as though there would be no
more questions to ask.

The Racial and Cultural Politics of Meat

Despite the limitations of Adams' approach, her argument remains important
in pointing to the ways in which eating animals might be linked to sexual
politics. Additionally, her project is useful because it reminds us, albeit much
more briefly, of the links between speciesism and racism. Adams does this by
pointing to the history of cannibalism, a term which derives from the Spanish
mispronunciation of people from the Caribbean:

As Europeans explored the continents of North and South America
and Africa, the indigenous peoples of those lands became accused of
cannibalism – the ultimate savage act. Once labelled as cannibals, their
defeat and enslavement at the hands of civilized, Christian whites
became justifiable . . . One cause of cannibalism was thought to be lack
of animal protein. Yet most Europeans themselves during the centuries
of European expansion were not subsisting on animal protein every
day. The majority of cultures in the world satisfied their protein needs
through vegetables and grains. By charging indigenous peoples with
cannibalism (and thus demonstrating their utterly savage ways, for they
supposedly did to humans what Europeans only did to animals) one
justification for colonization was provided. (2010: 54–5)

Adams here exposes a double myth that is used to justify violence towards animals and towards other humans: that meat eating is a requirement for a healthy body and has always been part of the human diet; and that non-Europeans choose to eat other human bodies and are therefore lesser humans. Adams goes so far as to say that 'racism is perpetuated each time meat is thought to be the best protein source'. This is because 'the emphasis on the nutritional strengths of animal protein distorts the dietary history of most cultures in which complete protein dishes were made of vegetables and grains' (54–5). The dominant western attitude towards eating animals means that the rich array of alternative non-meat culinary traditions are marginalised within wider cultural norms that are so prevalent as to seem natural.

As soon as the practice of eating meat is de-naturalised, however, we have to pay attention to the locations in which thinking about animal ethics is situated. Postcolonial animal theorists have suggested, for example, that it is important to foreground race and cultural differences as much as gender in feminist discussions of animals in order to avoid essentialism, ethnocentrism and elitism. Too often this is not the case, and the '"Universal Woman" of white, Western feminist theory has made more than a problematic appearance' in contemporary debates about animal ethics (Deckha 2012: 529). The disproportionate attention paid to the voice of white western feminists is problematic because it doesn't allow for a critique of the way that eating in non-western contexts may have a different impact on sexual politics. What it means to eat meat as a woman and as a man may be different, but it is just as important to take into account what it means to eat meat as a woman or a man in different cultures. This is a point underlined by the feminist animal theorist Cathryn Bailey:

> What it means to be an African American vegetarian likely differs
> from what it means to be an Iranian vegetarian or a white American
> vegetarian. The point is that these identities are shaped by . . .
> ideological forces . . .: the association of oppressed groups with
> animality; the various connections between the oppression of human
> and nonhuman animals; the construction of gender, race, class, nation,
> and imperialism (and resistance to it as well) through the raising,
> butcher, transport, and eating of animals; the political economies of
> food access and food security; and the everyday reinscription of white
> supremacy and gender inequalities through the ingestion of meat and
> what it means. (2007: 57)

The aim here is not to revert to a form of moral relativism where anything goes, but rather to more carefully and rigorously account for the contextual structures that play a crucial role in oppression across sexual, racial, class and national lines.

The racial politics of eating meat is at its darkest, according to Marjorie Spiegel, when we consider the shared exploitation of animals and human slaves. Her 1988 book *The Dreaded Comparison* is full of examples of where racism and speciesism meet. Where slaves are treated 'like animals', we might say that both, to borrow Adams' term, become absent referents. Such figurative language conceals a shared oppression where the animals' plight is not commonly acknowledged as unethical in the same way that slavery now is: 'we have decided that treatment which is wholly unacceptable when received by a human being is in fact the proper manner in which to treat a non-human animal' (Spiegel 1996: 19). With regards to the issue of eating animals, the circulation of livestock in global capitalist markets, where they are transported around the world in severely cramped conditions only to be auctioned and slaughtered on arrival, disturbingly mirrors the 'hellish' treatment of slaves in the 'Middle Passage' as they were transported to the 'New World' (52). Hidden behind figurative language *and* materially hidden from human view, the world is filled with factory farms and slaughterhouses that perpetuate 'animal slavery' where 'secrecy is necessary to keep the system intact' (82). Just as with Adams' argument, it is of course important to note the very different contexts and consequences of violence towards humans and animals (28). In beginning to do so, Spiegel's book once again exposes the secretive exploitation of animals and the hypocrisies in human attitudes towards violence and oppression.

The complexity of intersections between sexist, racist and speciesist oppression is still being worked through by animal theorists. Taking account of how such socio-cultural issues matter to the question of eating animals cautions against the view that ethics is ever settled or universal; animal ethics is instead revealed as an ongoing process of thought as well as of action. Even within those cultures that groups of people presume to share, the actors involved in the process of eating or not eating meat are many and complex, and the ways in which animals become meat vary. As Diamond reminds us, 'eating animals . . . is not just one thing' (1978: 471). We see this complexity in an anecdote Haraway shares in her 'Parting Bites' at the end of *When Species Meet*. Haraway recalls a meal she had with her academic colleagues and her uneasiness in siding with any one ethical position – she seeks to avoid 'hostile polemic', 'dogmatic purity' or, for that matter, 'easy relativism' (2008: 296). The host, religion studies scholar Gary Lease, a hunter as well as environmentalist, roasted a feral pig (a species Haraway stresses are 'highlight intelligent, opportunistic, socially adept, well armed, and emotionally talented' [297]) in his garden in California. In a provocative passage, Haraway writes:

> Hunting, killing, cooking, serving, and eating (or not) a pig is a very
> intimate personal and public act at every stage of the process, with

major consequences for a community that cannot be – and should
not be – composed along the lines of organic holism. Several diners
in Lease's yard that spring not only refused to eat the succulent pork
he served but also argued passionately that he was out of line to serve
hunted meat. They argued that his kind of hospitality was an act of
aggression not only to the animals but also to the students and faculty.
The department should adopt a vegan practice, they maintained, or at
least a practice that did not include the community's facing the body
of a whole animal for collective consumption. But feral pigs, hunters,
eaters, and resisters are companion species, entangled in a messy meal
with no sweet desert to settle everybody's digestion . . . What is to be
done, if neither liberal relativism nor the fiat of the self-certain of any
stripe is a legitimate option? (298–9)

As a result of this argument hunted pig was never cooked and served again for
the department. They 'all avoided conflict' and 'no real collective engagement
on the ways of life and death at stake took place' (299).

What Haraway bemoans is not an ethical position of right and wrong, so
much as the loss of a potential ethical encounter. To be sure, the aim of such
encounters is not to resolve contradictory positions – those against and for
eating animals – but rather to forge modes of 'action and respect without
resolution' that carefully account for the complex dynamics present when
species eat and are eaten (300). Eating is a communal event, and if we cease
to eat together we cease to engage with the alternative worldviews that 'arise
when people respond to seriously different, felt and known, finite truths and
must cohabit well without a final peace' (299). For Haraway the ethics located
at the table is as important as what is *on* the table. Only by being willing to
challenge, and be challenged by, the people sitting opposite us at the table can
ethics become more important than etiquette. For all that human language has
been seen to divide humans and animals, this language needs to be used anew
to engage with different people in different contexts about animal ethics. The
real mark of human arrogance would be to have the last word.

MEAT STORIES: *EATING ANIMALS*

Dinner tables are full of stories. It is a scenario many readers of this book will
have witnessed: a group of family or friends are sitting in a restaurant and,
when ordering, attention focuses on the person looking for vegetarian options.
A conversation (at times bordering on an interrogation) ensues. When did
you become vegetarian? What made you stop eating meat? Do you still eat
fish...(!)? On the one hand the repetition of this kind of scenario, and these

questions, speaks to a human curiosity about that which is different and illustrates that the choice not to eat meat is still far from a cultural norm. But it also shows how the issue of eating meat remains divisive, where culinary preferences are reduced to oppositional categories of those who do and those who don't eat animals. All too often the stories we *could* tell at the table are quashed by dogmatism or ignorance.

In his 2009 book *Eating Animals*, Jonathan Safran Foer argues that the choice of whether or not to eat meat is too often understood within an 'all-or-nothing' framework where there is little room for nuance or complication: 'never eat them or never sincerely question eating them; become an activist or disdain activists' (2009: 32). Rather than seeking to enter the complex and at times contradictory space in between these two positions, the polarised difference can even lead to assumptions about entire lifestyles:

> It's a way of thinking that we would never apply to other ethical realms.
> (Imagine always or never lying.) I can't count the times that upon
> telling someone I am vegetarian, he or she responded by pointing out
> an inconsistency in my lifestyle or trying to find a flaw in an argument
> I never made. (I have often felt that my vegetarianism matters more to
> such people than it does to me.) (32–3)

The disparaging fascination that meat eaters have for vegetarianism betrays a paradox in the 'choice-obsessed modern West' where 'ironically, the utterly unselective omnivore – "I'm easy; I'll eat anything" – can appear more socially sensitive than the individual who tries to eat in a way that is good for society'. Such undiscerning food choices are rarely based on 'reason (even consciousness)' (32–3); meat eating seems instead to be a kind of learned instinct: it has become a seemingly natural process to the extent that we don't even have to make the choice at all. The very thing that is so often used by people to distinguish humans from animals – namely, reason – suddenly departs when humans are faced with the prospect of eating those animals.

Foer's book makes the inconveniently reasonable claim that meat eating as practised in western countries today – and especially in the United States – is not natural. Evidence of this is found in the ways in which habits have changed dramatically in the course of the last century. We have never before eaten as much meat as we do now, and some of the statistics *Eating Animals* presents are startling: 'On average, Americans eat the equivalent of 21,000 entire animals in a lifetime'; 'All told, farmed animals in the United States produce 130 times as much waste as the human population – roughly 87,000 pounds of shit *per second*' (174); 'Animal agriculture makes a 40% greater contribution to global warming than all transportation in the world combined' and is therefore 'the number one cause of climate change' (43); 'For each food animal species, animal agriculture is now dominated by the factory farm – 99.9 percent of chickens raised for meat, 97 percent of laying hens, 99 percent of turkeys, 95 percent of pigs, 78 percent of cattle' (109); 'Globally, roughly 50 billion land animals are now factory farmed every year. (There is no tally of fish)' (34). The figures grow to disturbing proportions, and yet 'no tally for fish' is perhaps the most shocking of all – the figure is so large, the practice so widespread, that it cannot be quantified. These statistics are made all the more perplexing by a survey which revealed '96 percent of Americans say that animals deserve legal protection, 76 percent say that animal welfare is more important to them than low meat prices, and nearly two-thirds advocate passing not only laws but "strict laws" concerning the treatment of farmed animals'. As Foer notes, 'you'd be hard pressed to find any other issue on which so many people see eye to eye' (73). How, then, does a social attitude that agrees we shouldn't be cruel to animals tally with a social practice where eating animals is seen as the most natural thing in the world?

One answer is that our choice to eat or not to eat animals (and often there is a distinct *lack* of choice on the menu) is often based on words rather than numbers. The problem is that frequently we come across words that are deliberately and cynically deployed to obscure the reality behind the statistics listed above:

> Language is never fully trustworthy, but when it comes to eating animals, words are as often used to misdirect and camouflage as they are to communicate. Some words, like *veal*, help us forget what we are actually talking about. Some, like *free-range*, can mislead those whose consciences seek clarification. Some, like *happy*, mean the opposite of what they would seem. And some, like *natural*, mean next to nothing. (45)

Echoing Carol Adams' argument that through language real animals become invisible, Foer explains how the realities of the lives and deaths of animals are hidden behind certain terms. The above passage comes from the first word, appropriately enough 'Animal', in an alphabet of terms *Eating Animals* discusses. This singular word, Foer reminds us, can never be taken to represent all animals in all places and all times. Context matters: 'Within a culture, even within a family, people have their own understandings of what an animal is. Within each of us there are probably several different understandings' (45). We can add that such conflicting views of what an 'animal' is extend to human beings: we are a part of the animal kingdom and yet often see ourselves as standing outside, or even above, it. The choice of whether to eat animals or not is therefore complicated by a multiplicity of conceptualisations.

There are a number of other words Foer warns us to be wary of. *Bycatch* 'refers to sea creatures caught by accident', including the numerous fish popu-lations that are devastated by shrimp trawling and tuna fishing. But these fish are not killed '"by accident," since bycatch has been consciously built into contemporary fishing methods' – to talk of 'bycatch' is therefore 'the quintes-sential example of bullshit' (49). *Free-range* often only signals some 'access to the outdoors' which could simply mean there is small door at one end of a shed containing thousands of chickens, or even a window that these animals can look out of. It doesn't, then, specify much about the actual conditions in which chickens are kept (61). *Fresh* really means poultry that 'has never had an internal temperature below 26 degrees or above 40 degrees Fahrenheit' and therefore 'fresh chicken can be frozen'. All of which means that 'Pathogen-infested, feces-splattered chicken can technically be fresh, cage-free, and free-range, and sold in the supermarket legally (the shit does need to be rinsed off first)' (61). And, as a further example, *Organic* signifies 'a whole lot less than we give it credit for' in that it may mean the animals haven't been fed crops with pesticides and fertilizers, or antibiotics or growth hormones, and that they have some 'access to the outdoors' which again can simply mean a window. 'Organic' *does* 'signal better welfare if we are talking about laying hens or cattle. It also *may* signal better welfare for pigs, but that is less certain.' But 'for chickens raised for meat and for turkeys' it 'doesn't necessarily mean any-thing in terms of welfare issues. You can call your turkey organic and torture it daily' (70). Clearly, when we encounter such words in relation to food we shouldn't allow them to comfort us or lull us into a complacent view that we are not part of the global networks of exploitation against animals. Rather than easing our consciences, these words should arouse our suspicion.

Facts and words therefore work against each other too often where eating animals is concerned. We may be outraged by the statistics listed above, but they can feel somewhat abstract and distanced from our everyday lives where we rarely encounter this suffering and death first-hand. Similarly, we are reas-sured by comforting words, but these words can distract us from the every-day lives and deaths of animals behind the statistics. In both cases – whether numbers or words – the focus is on neatly packaged, easily (mis)understood quantities and categories. Missing are qualitative, hitherto unrecognised *stories* about eating animals, and for Foer 'eating and storytelling are inseparable'. There are many stories to be told about 'what meat *is*' and that might engage a host of important questions: 'Where does it come from? How is it produced? How are animals treated, and to what extent does that matter? What are the economic, social, and environmental effects of eating animals?' (12). The problem is that we 'smudge, diminish, and forget' that there are stories relat-ing to such questions behind the numbers and the words (7). Stories can help find ways to make the statistics and words speak to each other: 'place facts in a story, a story of compassion or domination, or maybe both – place them in a story about the world we live in and who we are and who we want to be – and you can begin to speak meaningfully about eating animals' (14). Telling the story of meat helps to put flesh on statistics and to wash the shit off the words often spoken.

Eating Animals does tell a story about the production and consumption of meat. In contrast to awkward dinner table conversations, or situations where, as Haraway describes above, all discussion is silenced, the story Foer tells allows a variety of actors within vast networks of the meat industry to speak. As the book progresses that story develops into multiple *stories* narrated by an activist (90–3), a factory farmer (94–7), a poultry farmer (110–15), a vegetarian farmer (205–10), and a vegan who is designing a mobile slaughterhouse (238–41) – each of which demands a response and each of which tells us something previously unrecognised. A complicated picture emerges that poses a challenge to neat, oppositional modes of thinking about animal ethics: 'ranchers can be vegetarians, vegans can build slaughterhouses, and I can be a vegetarian who supports the best of animal agriculture' (242). Foer shows how it is possible to have a strong argument about eating animals which is also a narrative of multiplicity. He writes of his personal experience and wider contexts without conflating the two:

> To decide for oneself and one's family is not to decide for the nation or the world . . . though I see value in all of us sharing our personal reflections and decisions about eating animals, I didn't write this book simply to reach a personal conclusion. Farming is shaped not only by food choices, but by political ones. Choosing a personal diet is insufficient. But how far am I willing to push my own decisions and my own views about the best alternative animal agriculture? . . . What should we all expect of one another when it comes to the question of eating animals? (198–9)

Eating Animals reveals the importance of telling collective stories rather than simply halting at the personal individual level of preference. To do so would be in danger of reaffirming the neoliberal model of choice that obscures the wider reality that we are not in fact choosing a different mode of living at all.

We need, then, to move past the idea of becoming consistent ethical individuals, which can actually mask a conservative privatism. Reflecting on his own hypocrisy or inconsistency (for example he drinks milk, which he claims involves more cruelty to animals than eating beef), Foer has remarked in an interview that 'we have to get away from the expectation of perfection because it really intimidates people who would otherwise make an effort. People use the fear of hypocrisy to justify total inaction' (2011). The real choice that needs to be opened up, and that is opened up by Foer's book, is between a simple oppositional stance, and a more complicated, nuanced understanding of meat-eating processes and practices. Crucially, in giving these nuanced positions voice, the book does what all the best stories do in demanding that we respond to that which we cannot see as much as to that which faces us every day.

One of the most powerful voices in *Eating Animals* comes from someone who kills certain animals for a living because of an ethical concern for other animals he will never come face-to-face with. Frank Reese is a poultry farmer who 'holds a special status' in that he is the one farmer Foer met who preserves 'traditional genetics' and 'doesn't do anything on his ranch that is plainly cruel' (2009: 234). His whole life's work is based on producing turkeys for consumption so that he might save other, less cared for, turkeys from the cruelty they experience in the dominant production processes of factory farming:

> Not a single turkey you can buy in a supermarket could walk normally,
> much less jump or fly. Did you know that? They can't even have
> sex. Not the antibiotic-free, or organic, or free-range, or anything.
> They all have the same foolish genetics, and their bodies won't allow
> for it anymore. Every turkey sold in every store and served in every
> restaurant was the product of artificial insemination. If it were only
> for efficiency, that would be one thing, but these animals literally can't
> reproduce naturally. (111, original in italics)

We have seen how Foer's book, like many of the theoretical texts discussed in this chapter, challenges the idea that consuming meat is a natural activity and instead reveals that it is a cultural practice. But a second level of de-naturalisation is apparent here in exposing the myth that we are eating 'animals' at all. In the twenty-first century many animals are artificially bred in such a way that they can't themselves breed. *That* demands a story.

KEY TEXTS

Adams, Carol J. (2010), *The Sexual Politics of Meat: A Feminist-Vegetarian Critical Theory*, 20th Anniversary Edition, London: Bloomsbury.

Derrida, Jacques (1991), '"Eating Well", or the Calculation of the Subject', in Eduardo Cadava, Peter Connor and Jean-Luc Nancy (eds), *Who Comes After the Subject*, New York: Routledge, pp. 96–119.

Derrida, Jacques (2004), 'Violence Against Animals', in Jacques Derrida and Elizabeth Roudinesco, *For What Tomorrow... A Dialogue*, trans. Jeff Fort, Stanford: Stanford University Press, pp. 62–76.

Derrida, Jacques (2008), *The Animal That Therefore I Am*, trans. David Wills, New York: Fordham University Press.

Derrida, Jacques (2009), *The Beast and the Sovereign*, vol. 1, trans. Geoffrey Bennington, Chicago: University of Chicago Press.

Diamond, Cora (1978), 'Eating Meat and Eating People', *Philosophy* 53:206, 465–79.

Foer, Jonathan Safran (2009), *Eating Animals*, London: Penguin.

Levinas, Emmanuel (1988), 'The Paradox of Morality: An Interview with Emmanuel Levinas', in Robert Bernasconi and David Wood (eds), *The Provocation of Levinas: Rethinking the Other*, trans. Andrew Benjamin, London: Routledge, pp. 168–80.

Levinas, Emmanuel (1989), 'Ethics as First Philosophy', in *The Levinas Reader*, ed. Sean Hand, Oxford: Blackwell, pp. 76–87.

Levinas, Emmanuel (2004), 'The Name of a Dog, or Natural Rights', in Peter Atterton and Matthew Calarco (eds), *Animal Philosophy: Ethics and Identity*, London: Continuum, pp. 47–50.

Haraway, Donna (2008), 'Parting Bites: Nourishing Indigestion', in *When Species Meet*, Minneapolis: University of Minnesota Press, pp. 285–301.

Nussbaum, Martha (2007), *Frontiers of Justice: Disability, Nationality, Species Membership*, Cambridge: Harvard University Press.

Regan, Tom (1983), *The Case for Animal Rights*, London: Routledge & Kegan Paul.

Singer, Peter (1995), *Animal Liberation*, Second Edition, London: Pimlico.

Singer, Peter (ed.) (2006), *In Defense of Animals: The Second Wave*, Oxford: Blackwell.

Spiegel, Marjorie (1996), *The Dreaded Comparison: Human and Animal Slavery*, New York: Mirror Books.

FURTHER READING

Adams, Carol J. and Josephine Donovan (eds) (1995), *Animals and Women: Feminist Theoretical Explorations*, Durham NC: Duke University Press.

Bailey, Cathryn (2007), 'We Are What We Eat: Feminist Vegetarianism and the Reproduction of Racial Identity', *Hypatia: A Journal of Feminist Philosophy* 22.2, 39–59.

Bailly, Jean-Christophe (2011), *The Animal Side*, trans. Catherine Porter, New York: Fordham University Press.

Beauvoir, Simone de. (1997), *The Second Sex*, trans. H. M. Parshley, London: Vintage.

Bentham, Jeremy (1982), *An Introduction to the Principles of Morals and Legislation*, London: Methuen.

Braidotti, Rosi (2013), 'Post-Humanism: Life Beyond the Self', in *The Posthuman*, Cambridge: Polity, pp. 13–54.

Calarco, Matthew (2008), 'The Passion of the Animal: Derrida', in *Zoographies: The Question of the Animal from Heidegger to Derrida*, New York: Columbia University Press, pp. 103–49.

Cavalieri, Paola (2001), *The Animal Question: Why Nonhuman Animals Deserve Human Rights*, trans. Catherine Woollard, Oxford: Oxford University Press.

Cavalieri, Paola (2009), *The Death of the Animal*, New York: Columbia University Press.

Deckha, Maneesha (2012), 'Toward a Postcolonial, Posthumanist Feminist Theory: Centralizing Race and Culture in Feminist Work on Nonhuman Animals', *Hypatia: A Journal of Feminist Philosophy*, 27.3, 527–45.

Fellenz, Marc R. (2007), *The Moral Menagerie: Philosophy and Animal Rights*, Urbana and Chicago: University of Illinois Press.

Foer, Jonathan Safran (2011), 'Interview: Ecologists Who Eat Meat Have a Blind Spot', *The Ecologist*, 24 January 2011; at <http://www.theecologist.org/Interviews/739796/jonathan_safran_foer_environmentalists_who_eat_meat_have_a_blindspot.html> (accessed 15 December 2014).

Gruen, Lori (2011), *Ethics and Animals: An Introduction*, Cambridge: Cambridge University Press.

Hearne, Vicki (1994), *Animal Happiness: A Moving Exploration of Animals and Their Emotions*, New York: Skyhorse Publishing.

Hegel, G. W. F. (1991), *Elements of the Philosophy of Right*, ed. Allen W. Wood, Cambridge: Cambridge University Press.

Irigaray, Luce (2004), 'Animal Compassion', in Peter Atterton and Matthew Calarco (eds), *Animal Philosophy: Ethics and Identity*, London: Continuum, pp. 195–201.

Kelley, Lindsay and Lynn Turner (eds) (2013), 'Special Issue: bon appétit', *Parallax* 19.1.

Lee, Paula Young (ed.) (2008), *Meat, Modernity, and the Rise of the Slaughterhouse*, Durham: University of New Hampshire Press.

Matheny, Gaverick (2006), 'Utilitarianism and Animals', in Peter Singer (ed.), *In Defense of Animals: The Second Wave*, Oxford: Blackwell, pp. 13–25.

Oliver, Kelly (2009), 'The Beaver's Struggle with Species-Being: De Beauvoir and the Praying Mantis', in *Animal Lessons: How They Teach Us to Be Human*, New York: Columbia University Press, pp. 155–74.

Otter, Chris (2008), 'Civilizing Slaughter: The Development of the British Public Abattoir, 1850–1910', in Paula Young Lee (ed.), *Meat, Modernity, and the Rise of the Slaughterhouse*, Durham: University of New Hampshire Press, pp. 89–106.

Pick, Anat (2011), *Creaturely Poetics: Animality and Vulnerability in Literature and Film*, New York: Columbia University Press.

Plutarch (2007), 'The Eating of Flesh', in Linda Kalof and Amy Fitzgerald (eds), *The Animals Reader: The Essential Classic and Contemporary Writings*, Oxford: Berg, pp. 154–7.

Rousseau, Jean-Jacques (1979), *Emile, or On Education*, trans. Allan Bloom, New York: Basic Books.

Ryder, Richard (1971), 'Experiments on Animals', in Stanley Godlovitch, Roslind Godlovitch and John Harris (eds), *Animals, Men and Morals: An Enquiry into the Maltreatment of Non-humans*, London: Victor Gollancz, pp. 41–82.

Steiner, Gary (2005), *Anthropocentrism and Its Discontents: The Moral Status of Animals in the History of Western Philosophy*, Pittsburgh: University of Pittsburgh Press.

The Animal Studies Group (2006), *Killing Animals*, Urbana and Chicago: University of Illinois Press.

Turner, Lynn (2013), 'Insect Asides', in *The Animal Question in Deconstruction*, Edinburgh: Edinburgh University Press.

Walters, Kerry S. and Lisa Portmess (eds) (1999), *Ethical Vegetarianism: From Pythagoras to Peter Singer*, Albany: State University of New York Press.

Wolfe, Cary (2008), 'Exposures', in Stanley Cavell, Cora Diamond, John McDowell, Ian Hacking and Cary Wolfe, *Philosophy and Animal Life*, New York: Columbia University Press, pp. 1–42.

Wolfe, Cary (2010), 'Flesh and Finitude: Bioethics and the Philosophy of the Living', in *What is Posthumanism?*, Minneapolis: University of Minnesota Press, pp. 49–98.

Wood, David (1999), 'Comment me pas manger – Deconstruction and Humanism', in H. Peter Steeves (ed.), *Animal Others: On Ethics, Ontology, and Animal Life*, Albany: State University of New York Press, pp. 15–36.

Index